Going For God

Milestones in the Christian Life

By D. Hinton

Questions Young People Ask

By D. Newell

Published by
JOHN RITCHIE LTD.,
40 Beansburn, Kilmarnock KA3 1RH

ISBN 0 946351 05 8

Copyright © 1986 by John Ritchie Ltd.,
40 Beansburn, Kilmarnock, Scotland

All rights reserved. No part of this publication may be reproduced,
stored in a retrieval system, or transmitted in any form or by any
other means — electronic, mechanical, photocopy, recording or
otherwise — without the prior permission of the copyright owner.

Typeset and printed by G.T.P., 48 York St., Glasgow.

Contents

Milestones in the Christian Life

By D. Hinton

Questions Young People Ask

By D. Newell

Introduction

THE two series of articles contained in this booklet were published in the Believers' Magazine in recent years. Requests have been received from believers in various parts of the world that the articles should be reprinted in booklet form; this has now been done.

The articles will be of value only if they are approached as being not the personal views of the brethren concerned but, as we sincerely believe, the teaching of the Word of God.

We trust that believers will not only ponder the issues involved in the light of Scripture but will also do all they can to bring the booklet to the notice of others.

> "Wherewithal shall a young man cleanse his way?
> By taking heed thereto according to thy word."
>
> Psalm 119:9

Salvation

There are a number of events in our lives which can be thought of as milestones. That is, they are important stages in our development because decisions taken at those points in time alter the whole course of our subsequent experience and usefulness. Yet we do not always appreciate at the time how vital the decisions are that we are making.

The most important of these milestones is salvation, for in the sight of God it is only then that we begin to live.

We need to be clear concerning the nature of salvation. It is not just believing in Jesus, or asking Him into one's heart. There must be some acknowledgment of the seriousness of one's sin in the sight of a holy God and a true faith that the Saviour's death on the cross of Calvary alone enables a sinner to be forgiven. As the apostle puts it, "repentance toward God and faith in our Lord Jesus Christ" (Acts 20:21).

Prior to salvation we had been dead in sins (Eph 2:1), in darkness and the grip of Satan (Col 1:13). At salvation our sins were erased and we received a new life. This not only fitted us for heaven (John 3:3) but also brought us into the family of God (John 1:12) and into the light of the kingdom of the Son of His love, our Lord Jesus Christ.

This transformation was a divine act in the realm of the spirit, but there was intended to be a corresponding change in our outward manner of life which all would see.

We became a "new creation" (2 Cor 5:17) at the very moment of our new birth, and this was to affect every aspect of our lives. Whether at home, school, college or work, all should have seen a difference in us from the time we were saved.

The Bible speaks of this change that is expected at salvation as "putting off the old man" (what we were by natural birth as the descendants of Adam) and putting on the "new" (what we are in Christ). What this means in practice is set out in Col 3:8-14 —a complete change in habits and character.

This was put another way when the Saviour said, "By their fruits ye shall know them" (Matt 7:20). Such fruit is the evidence in the life of the character of the Saviour. Thus He clearly states that it is not words of profession that prove salvation but its manifestation in the life.

Now, just as we could not be saved by our own efforts, so as believers we cannot live as we ought by our own strength. To meet our need in this respect we were indwelt at salvation by the Holy Spirit, Himself a co-equal member of the Godhead. He came then in all His fulness and we can never have more of Him than we received then.

If we permit Him, He will prompt our hearts and consciences to do the things we ought. Moreover, with His power within, there is no excuse for any of us failing to glorify our Father. Being born into the divine family we should desire to act in such a way that He is pleased and glorified, not doing anything that would bring shame upon Him.

As we read the Scriptures, the sacred, inspired Word of God, the Spirit will impress upon us the things which He knows we need at that time. We must, of course, read with an open mind and heart, not with preconceived ideas.

As we grow spiritually by taking divine food, we should appreciate, to an even greater extent, both what we have been saved from and the price paid for our salvation. If this is so it will bring an ever increasing desire to live to the glory of our Saviour and to please Him in all things.

We have, in the history of the children of Israel, an illustration of the change of position that salvation brings and the consequential change in life expected by God. In Egypt they were at one stage under the judgment of Jehovah, just like the Egyptians. Then, having been sheltered by the blood they were expected to live differently, as typified in the ordinance of the seven-day feast of unleavened bread. This indicated that they were to be a different people from the day of redemption— that was their beginning in the sight of God (Exod 12:2); and the same applies to each one of us. Leaven speaks of evil, and all that is evil is to be put away.

Thus this milestone of salvation is connected with decisions. Are our lives to be lived henceforth to the glory of God? Are we to make the Scriptures the sole guide and arbiter in our lives? Are we to seek to show our Saviour's character to those we live and work amongst?

Or are our lives to be lived for ourselves, forgetting the cost of salvation? Are we to ignore the Word of God and follow the world's wisdom? Are we to give the world a false impression of the character of our Lord?

It is recognised that most of us did not realise at

the moment of salvation the full implications of the step we were taking, or the extent of the blessing into which we had come. Many of us look back over years to that day and the challenge is, how far have we lived out that which we then professed? However much we have failed, now is the time to put matters right before the Lord, so that we may not be ashamed before Him at His coming.

We would encourage younger readers especially to face up to these challenges. If our Lord does not soon return life will pass by swiftly, and it is true that only what is done for His glory will last. Our response to these possibilities will decide the usefulness of our lives to the Lord—how sad to look back in future years and regret wrong decisions leading to wasted lives.

Baptism

We come now to the second milestone in the life of a believer—or what our Lord intended should be the second for us all. Salvation was a spiritual experience unseen by men, a transaction with a holy God; baptism is principally a practical experience, a witness before men of what has occurred in secret between us and God.

Has each reader passed this milestone? For it is very definitely the will of our Saviour that baptism should closely follow salvation. If we have not passed this point in the divine pathway set out for us, why not?

How thankful we should be that the ordinances the Lord has enjoined upon us can be fulfilled by all, brethren and sisters, young and old, irrespective of gift or education. Moreover in this ordinance we are privileged to follow the example of our Lord Himself, who was baptised in Jordan.

That all those who have passed the first milestone of salvation should come to the second is clear from His words in Matt 28:19, "make disciples of all nations, baptising them". This injunction was clearly followed in apostolic times. From Pentecost onward baptism followed every recorded case of salvation. This reminds us that baptism should form an integral part of the preaching of the gospel. Philip must have taught baptism to the eunuch in Acts 8.

Baptism is derived from a Greek verb meaning "to dip". It speaks of total immersion in, submersion under, and emergence from a liquid. It cannot be interpreted in any other way. Sprinkling in no way meets the meaning of Scripture, indeed it denies the very truth of which baptism speaks. The word was used by the Greeks with reference to dyeing a bale of cloth. The bale had to be totally immersed in the new colour for the dye to be effective. Baptism always took place in water in the Scriptures, proving it was not a spiritual experience. John, we read in John 3:23, baptised where there was much water. The Ethiopian eunuch went down into and came up out of the water.

Baptism was not meant to apply only to Jewish believers. Cornelius, the Roman centurion, and the eunuch demonstrate this, fulfilling the Lord's commission which embraced "all nations".

We are not told to wait until we fully understand the implications of baptism—we shall never reach that state. None of those whose baptism is recorded in the Acts could have appreciated all the meaning of what they were doing. They were not asked to wait a probationary period or to pass an examination.

Furthermore we can never excuse ourselves by saying that we are waiting until the Lord tells us to be baptised. He has already told us in His Word in the clearest terms and He will say no more.

Do you feel it is sufficient that you were baptised as an infant? Such a thought ignores the whole teaching of Scripture on the subject: baptism follows salvation as the result of a deliberate request by the person concerned. It is a public witness to what happened when we were saved; how then can it take place before salvation? We are immersed in water to show our identification with our Saviour in His death and burial. We come out of the water to show our identification with Him in resurrection life, thereafter to walk before others in "newness of life" (Rom 6:4).

Baptism has no part in our salvation, nor is it just a passport to membership of a company of believers. Sad to say we may be saved and yet not baptised; even sadder, we may be baptised and yet not saved. However, baptism should precede being added to a company of believers, following the example of Acts 2:4-42, for how otherwise can we be seen to be following the apostles' doctrine?

The meaning of baptism is illustrated at the crossing of Jordan by the Israelites under Joshua (Josh 3, 4). Only through the ark going in front of them, in picture going down into the waters of death, could the nation go across on dry ground. The nation was represented by twelve stones set up in the bed of the river to identify the people with the place the ark of the covenant had taken. Another twelve stones set up at Gilgal (Josh 4:20) spoke of the "reproach of Egypt" being rolled away—the old life was over, a new life with new associations was beginning.

By the Saviour's death judgment has been averted for the believer. In baptism we confess that we should have been judged but that He took our place. Just as Israel was intended to remember those stones in the river all their days, so baptism was meant to have a lasting effect on our lives. In moments of temptation we are to remember the time when we took our place publicly with a crucified Saviour.

Why should baptism be considered an important

milestone in our lives?

Firstly it is the first test as to whether our profession of allegiance to the Lord was real; submission to Him in baptism is an evidence of spiritual life. Contrariwise, a refusal to obey Him in this way, after one has been shown the scriptural teaching on the subject, raises doubts as to whether He really is our Lord, for if He is we will gladly bow our will to His commands. Salvation includes confessing Him as Lord (Rom 8:10), baptism demonstrates this publicly.

In the second place our spiritual growth is stunted, and may, be halted, if we wilfully disregard the Lord's wishes in this matter.

Thirdly, by taking this public stand one is "nailing one's colours to the mast", showing where one's loyalties lie. It is the great dividing line in the eyes of the world. Even the unsaved recognise to some extent that those who are baptised are marking themselves out as a different people. Thus, in the days of persecution baptism was a signal for martyrdom. This is still the case in some lands hostile to the gospel.

The fourth reason is that baptism, although a unique experience, was intended to have a lasting effect upon us. Its teaching was never to be forgotten, especially in times of temptation.

Finally, if we are prepared to set aside the Lord's commandment on this subject, then this will affect our attitude to all the injunctions contained in the Scriptures. It is a test of our willingness to bow to the authority of the Word of God.

Reception

It was always the purpose of God that His redeemed people should be brought together into companies. This is vital for the purpose of witness but even more so because we cannot stand on our own. We need the companionship of those of a like mind, and therefore we are exhorted not to forsake the assembling of ourselves together (Heb 10:25).

Therefore it is not enough for you to have passed the milestones of salvation and baptism—the Saviour then expects you to join a company of believers gathering according to Scripture.

Now joining such a company does not mean just having one's name entered on a register of members, nor being allowed to participate in the Lord's Supper. You are not received to the breaking of bread but to the assembly of believers.

We commonly speak of coming into fellowship, but Scripture speaks of those already in fellowship being added to the number of the existing company. In other words, you should seek to be added to believers whose teaching you are already submitting to in principle. Those breaking bread in Acts 2:42 had already demonstrated that they were in fellowship by their submission to the apostles' teaching.

So you must seek out an autonomous group of born again believers gathering under the Lordship of Christ and responsible to Him alone.

Where Christ is Lord the sole criterion used in arriving at decisions is conformity to the Word of

God. The believers will not be part of any human organisation and will be led, not by a paid officer, but by elders, or shepherds.

Such a company is very precious to God, being bought with "the blood of His Own" (Acts 20:28, J.N.D). To join such a gathering is a great privilege; you must constantly bear in mind its preciousness to God, and therefore never do or say anything that will spoil or damage it. Such assemblies are not a sect or denomination, for such gatherings have been in existence since Pentecost, not just since the early part of the last century. It is the breaking away from the divinely-given principles of the New Testament that produces man-made sects and denominations.

Again we would emphasise that joining an assembly is not just participating in the Lord's Supper. You become a member of a body (1 Cor 12:18), and as such have a responsibility towards all the other members. Only by all working in harmony can the body function effectively. Scripture makes it clear that your every action will affect all the other members, either for good or ill.

To be in such a local body or assembly will be a unique experience. It is a partnership, irrespective of age, nationality or social status, a fellowship in the sorrows and joys of all the members and in every aspect of their activities. You will probably not be able to engage personally in all of these but you must be prayerfully concerned for them all.

Moreover, you must be prepared to accept the part in the company that you are given for your sphere of service. You have no right to expect to get your own way in these things, and are not to try to take over the responsibilities of others or to think that certain functions are beneath your dignity.

An assembly is not a democracy in which you have a vote. Its purpose is to manifest the pre-eminence and supremacy of Christ as Lord. Voting would destroy that picture. You will look for guidance to the elders or shepherds who will be responsible to the risen Lord alone. The word *elders* refers to their spiritual maturity and experience, whilst *shepherds* applies to their work, that of caring for the believers in all the ways that a shepherd cares for his flock.

They are not dictators, "lords over the heritage" (1 Pet 5:3), but are to lead the flock by example "as among them". They are not chosen by vote or on the basis of their professional qualifications or business experience. They are marked out by the Holy Spirit when they are seen to be carrying out the work of a shepherd, their way of life being measured by 1 Tim 3.

You are to obey the elders (Heb 13:17). When seeking to join an assembly you should expect to be questioned by them as to the reality of your fellowship. They have a responsibility to guard the assembly from any who would try to enter with the purpose of dividing or bringing wrong doctrine, or those who cannot be received on the basis of 1 Cor 5:11.

You must not therefore assume that because you have passed the second milestone of baptism you will automatically be received. Baptism depends on a profession of salvation alone; reception depends on one's preparedness to submit to the apostles doctrine and on one's manner of life.

When received into such an assembly you must ensure that there is nothing in your behaviour that will bring shame upon it. Angels are watching and expecting to see the Scriptures obeyed and the Lord exalted. So the brethren should have their heads uncovered in all the gatherings whilst the sisters will cover theirs, thus demonstrating the headship of Christ (1 Cor 11:3-10), and will keep silent (1 Cor 14:34). Remember that these principles do not apply just to the Lord's Supper; if you really desire Him to be set forth as Lord you will not try to find reasons for not complying.

The assembly, that is the believers themselves, form God's house (1 Tim 3:15), not the building in which you meet. Taking your place in His house you must appreciate that it is a holy place; therefore your conduct should be characterised by reverential awe. In the presence chamber of the eternal God you should dress and behave accordingly, for it is a far greater honour than attending Buckingham Palace.

Becoming part of this body, this house, various privileges will be opened up to you and at the same time corresponding responsibilities. You will have the privilege of remembering the Lord at His Supper and of serving Him; you will have the responsibility of protecting and preserving the assembly and its reputation.

Let us make it our aim that the scripturally-based local assembly may be as precious to us as it is to our God.

The Assembly Gatherings

Further important milestones in our spiritual lives are reached when attending the various meetings for the first time as one of the assembly. Brethren and sisters alike have a personal involvement and responsibility as part of the local believers. It is assumed that we will be present at all gatherings if at all possible; otherwise the reality of our fellowship will be questionable.

It is important that one comes to these gatherings in the right attitude. The Lord is present and therefore there should be reverence and godly behaviour. The Holy Spirit desires to control, so there should be a submission of our wills to His leading; this will not be possible where there is unconfessed sin.

It is wrong to think that we ever come just to sit and listen. The whole body is engaging itself in these exercises, and every member of that body, young and old, whether prominent or not, audible or silent, has a function to fulfil. It is too easy, especially in a large company, for one to be content to be an onlooker, a mere passenger.

Turning to the Gospel Meeting first, this is the focal point of the gospel outreach of the assembly. The aim of all other outreach should be that ultimately unsaved souls are brought to this gathering. It is not in itself the fulfilment of the command to go into all the world and preach the gospel. That necessitates going out, not waiting for folk to come in.

The Gospel Meeting should have figured much in our prayers during the preceding week, that the speaker would be guided by the Spirit, not just as to his subject but also as to the very words to be used. Furthermore the Lord should be pleaded with to prepare the hearts of those who will be present to receive His Word, whilst all should have done their utmost to tell unsaved souls of the meeting. During the meeting we should continue to be prayerful but at the same time listen intently to the speaker so as to encourage others to listen. All should act in a reverent and quiet manner, especially at the close when the Holy Spirit may be dealing with seeking souls.

The Prayer Meeting is held for the purpose of praying, collectively laying hold upon God. This is a great privilege, obtained as a result of the Saviour's death, and is not to be despised. All are to come to pray fervently, having made sure all sin has been confessed (Jas 5:16), for it is the prayer of a righteous believer that prevails. The sisters will pray silently, for it is the brethren (lit. the males) that are to pray audibly (1 Tim 2:8); but the prayers of male and female are equally effective. Prayer should be specific and in faith, believing that God will answer.

The Prayer Meeting recorded in Acts 4:24-30 is worthy of study. They had all gathered to pray, for they spoke with "one voice", which also signifies their unity of purpose. They were concerned for the glory of God; they did not ask for divine intervention to make things easier for themselves, but that they might be strengthened to preach the Word and demonstrate the power of the Name of the Lord. Prayer is never to be just for our freedom from problems and pain but always for the glory of God. Then we shall be truly able to ask in His Name, that is we shall be seeking what He would seek in the same circumstances.

We must be careful not to pray for others to do what we are not prepared to do ourselves. It is of no avail to pray that tracting will be done if we are not making ourselves available.

Elijah's prayer (Jas 5:17) is another example to be considered. Knowing the Word of God, he based his prayer on Deut 11:17; the prayer that prevails will always rest upon the character and promises of God. Remember the prayer of Abraham in Gen 18:25 and that of Moses in Exod 32:12. This is one very important reason for reading and memorising the whole Word of God. Prayer, however, is not the medium for revealing to others our knowledge of the Scriptures, nor are we heard for our lengthy praying. So never be afraid to pray briefly; Solomon's prayer at the dedication of the Temple (2 Chron 6) takes only some seven minutes to read.

In the English language we have the great privilege of being able to testify to the uniqueness of our God by reserving for Him the pronouns Thee, Thou and Thine, so as not to bring Him down to the level of men. Not to avail ourselves of this privilege is to slight our God.

Now it is clear from Acts 2:42 that if our attitude to the Lord's Supper and the Prayer Meeting is right, then all else will be in order, for service is not mentioned in these verses; it is an inevitable consequence of a right attitude to those matters. The corollary is that if we are not right on these

fundamentals, then however busy we are in the
service of our Lord He will not be able to bless it as
He would wish.

Turning to the gatherings of believers for the
exposition of God's Word, whether by way of
ministry or Bible Reading, these are to be approached
in an expectant attitude, believing that the Lord will
have a message for us. We must have opened ears to
allow His Word to sink down into our innermost
being. In this way we will be gradually moulded into
the likeness of our Lord in character. We come to
learn, not to give.

All that we hear should be proved at home by
personal meditation and study of the Scriptures.
This was the example set by the believers at Berea
(Acts 17:11), for which they received divine
commendation. We will never be able to offer the
excuse at the judgment seat that we were wrongly
taught. Even the youngest believer has an unction,
an anointing, that enables him to discern between
right and wrong if he is sincerely seeking the
Spirit's guidance.

May each reader pause to consider honestly
whether he is fulfilling his responsibilities both
Godward and manward in regard to the assembly
gatherings.

The Lord's Supper

One of the privileges of being a member of an assembly is that of keeping the Lord's Supper, and our first celebration of it is a definite milestone in our spiritual experience.

It was to be a weekly supper—the events of Acts 20 indicate this—and we will surely avail ourselves of the first opportunity we have to keep it. The intention of it being a weekly supper was both to keep the Lord very fresh in our minds and to ensure that we examine ourselves before the Lord each week.

We are to keep this supper on the first day of the week, thus beginning the new week with it. It should have priority over everything else including service, giving the Lord the first place.

The purpose of the supper is to remember the Lord (1 Cor 11:24), to call Him to mind in His eternal glory, birth, life, death, ascension and coming glory. It is not just to be occupied with His death, although that will be the focal point of it. As our thoughts dwell on these things our hearts are to be lifted in praise and thanksgiving to the Father through the Son (Heb 13:15; 1 Pet 2:5).

We cannot start calling Him to mind at the time the gathering commences. We should have been occupied with Him during the previous seven days, so that the Holy Spirit can bring to our minds those aspects for which He wishes us to give thanks. It is not a time for making much of our blessings—the Lord alone is to be extolled. How we have spent our

Saturday evening will affect our ability to worship
on the Lord's Day morning.

We are exhorted to examine ourselves and then
eat, after anything that needs to be confessed has
been put right (1 Cor 11:28). This is written to
those in fellowship, not for those seeking to be
added to the company. It was intended to ensure
that all matters were put right before we ate, both
with the Lord and with our brethren. If this is not
done there is no harmony between ourselves and
the Lord, and we make a mockery of the truth of
"the communion" of the body and blood of the Lord
(1 Cor 10). If this examination is carried out
honestly then no evil will be able to take root in our
lives.

As we gather to this supper, with Him in the
midst, our attitude should be one of reverence and
godly fear. For we gaze upon bread and wine,
symbols of the very body and blood of the Lord
Himself. We must stress that they are only
symbols, and never change their physical character.
Nevertheless we should behave as though His
actual body and blood were before us. How this
would solemnise our remembrance and concentrate
our thoughts if we only practised it. Having one's
eyes closed is a great help to centring one's mind on
the Lord and prevents distraction by other believers.

This is the one gathering when we all come to
give, not to receive. Brethren and sisters alike are
involved in the giving, and gift does not enter into
it. The brethren who lead the company audibly are
not to voice their own pet ideas but, burdened by
the Spirit with the glories of their Lord, utter
thanksgiving for Him that will express the hearts of

the company.

It is not an occasion for showing how much we know of the Scriptures or how accomplished we may be as orators. Nor should we come having decided beforehand what we will say. It is not a ministry meeting, although the reading of appropriate Scriptures will enhance our worship.

The time will come when we will partake of the loaf and drink of the cup—very solemn acts. The loaf represents His unique body which He entered into at Bethlehem, in which He lived a sinless life to the pleasure of the Father (Luke 9:35) and in which He bore the wrath of a holy God on account of sin. The more we appreciate the value of the life lived in that body, the more we will value the life laid down on the cross.

The bread which we eat is "the communion of the body of Christ" (1 Cor 10:16). Communion means fellowship or partnership. It speaks of a joint participation with Him in every department of our lives. This is illustrated in James and John being partners with Simon in fishing (Luke 5:10). We should therefore seek to live as He lived, and our attitude to sin should be His. It is the truth of "I am crucified with Christ" (Gal 2:20).

However, as we break the one loaf we show our fellowship, our oneness, with all the others breaking bread. How hypocritical then to break bread if we are not on speaking terms with one of them, or if we have wronged others or are undermining the teaching of the elders.

The cup pictures the precious blood of the Saviour, the exceeding precious blood of Christ. Blood is not only the basis of our redemption (Eph

1:7) but is also the basis of the fulfilment of all the divine purposes. The more we realise this, the more valuable the blood, the token of the life laid down, will be to us. Again the cup is "the communion of the blood of Christ". We have a part in all the blessings following from it, but we are to remember that we are a blood-sprinkled people, linked with the altar, wherever we go.

We have a solemn warning in Israel's history. Sprinkled with the blood in Exod 24:8, in covenant relationship with Jehovah, they soon left Him out of their thoughts and made the golden calf. Inevitably judgment followed.

At Corinth the keeping of the Supper had become a sham. There was no acknowledgment of the Lordship of Christ, and again judgment ensued (1 Cor 11:30).

In His mercy our God does not judge in the same way today, else who of us would remain? Yet He still hates that which is merely formal or is contrary to His Word, and as a result His blessing may be withheld.

May this Supper become increasingly precious to us as we keep it each week "till He come".

Leaving School

What a great milestone it is when we leave school and life opens out before us. Then, probably more than at any other time, decisions have to be made affecting our whole future. So it is very important that the believer makes such decisions in harmony with the mind of God.

Remember that Abram did not seek Jehovah's mind before going to Egypt (Gen 12:10), nor regarding bearing seed through Hagar (Gen 16:1); the disastrous consequences are being felt in world politics even today.

David normally sought divine guidance and Jehovah never failed him. However when he failed to do so, trouble inevitably followed, such as when he went down to Gath (1 Sam 27). On this visit it appears he added to his wives the mother of Absalom, with all the tragic consequences. So we must take care not to blindly follow our natural inclinations.

Probably the first decision at this time is whether to proceed either to college or university or to seek employment.

Now the Lord has planned for His people to be in all walks of life so that the divine character will be revealed in all spheres. He would have some of His people take one step, some another. Each will be equally valuable in His sight, each equally essential for the fulfilment of His purposes, provided that we make the right choice.

A degree should carry no weight among the

people of God, either as regards service or in the
administration of the affairs of the assembly.
Manual employment can be just as God honouring
as a professional career.

To know His will we must be sincere in our
praying. If we have made up our minds beforehand
it is hypocritical to ask His will. This was the sin of
the Jewish remnant in Jeremiah's day (Jer 42:40),
the sin of hypocrisy. We must say honestly with the
apostle, "What wilt thou have me to do?"

If we are to find employment we must ascertain
what He intends us to do with our lives. We will
surely not wish to be employed in matters which we
cannot share with our Lord. Careers that cater for
the soulish side of man, such as entertainment and
sport, must be ruled out together with those
occupations where trickery or misrepresentation
are involved. Nor should we even consider anything
that could stumble others in their spiritual life or
harm the unsaved. So we should not work in a
brewery or anywhere associated with strong drink.

The armed forces attract many because of the
sense of adventure and world-wide travel. But
should a believer place himself in a position where
he may have to take life? Can we seriously
contemplate the Lord doing so? If He would not,
how can we?

We will surely wish to devote our energies to the
work of the assembly, so those spheres where
frequent shift work will prevent our regular
attendance at the assembly gatherings or prevent
our undertaking responsibility in the activities of
the assembly need to be approached with great
care. These things must be weighed honestly in the

presence of the Lord.

Nevertheless, having written the above, there is still a wide choice of occupations remaining. We must not just ask His will and leave it all to Him, but must ourselves be looking for something to be impressed on our minds that would give an indication of His wishes. Even in the reading of a list of advertisements for posts it can be brought home to our hearts very vividly that a certain job is the right opening.

Once we are assured of the right course, then our application for the position must be an honest one. From the start we must decide that we will be honest in all things, whatever the price to be paid. Only thus can we expect our God to lead us.

On the other hand, if we are assured that it is the Lord's will that we should apply for entrance to a college or university, the first question is, To what establishment should we apply.

Here again academic requirements must not be the chief criteria. The course we feel He would have us take will greatly restrict the choice, but surely the nearness of the college to an assembly of the Lord's people is the first requisite. Is there transport on the Lord's Day early enough for us to attend the Lord's Supper? Will we be able to return after the weeknight meetings? How sad when young believers attend places of learning isolated from any assembly gathering. What profit is there if we come successfully through our course but lose our spiritual health in the process? No, if we are to please our God and know His help in our studies we must ensure that we can gather with His people on every possible occasion.

Having been accepted it would be well before we
arrive to decide our order of priorities. The course
is costly and is largely financed by other people, so it
must not be wasted; we are there to study. Yet the
meetings of the assembly must not be forsaken. So
whilst we should encourage and help all other
student believers, and seek to bring unbelievers
into the blessing of salvation, this should never be
done at the expense of meeting with the assembly.

The rules of the institution must be obeyed. The
college authorities are among the "powers that be"
mentioned in Rom 13:1. Neither should we join in
politics or demonstrations, for "our citizenship is in
heaven" (Phil 3:20 R.V.).

We must determine to stand for the whole truth
of God—the inspiration of the complete Word of
God, the deity and sinlessness of the Saviour, the
reality of heaven and hell and of eternal punishment
are but a few examples. Error must be opposed,
including such specious theories as evolution.
There can be no middle path in such matters.

All moral standards are being thrown overboard
today, but the injunction is still, "Keep thyself
pure" (I Tim. 5:22). Treat the opposite sex
courteously but not lightly, for frivolous behaviour
is not becoming to the citizens of heaven.

The student who approaches his future in this
way will surely know the blessing of the Lord on his
studies, his work and his spiritual life.

Starting Work

In most of our lives there comes the milestone when, for the first time, we enter employment. Until then we will probably have led a sheltered life to some extent but now will take our place in the outside world.

Certain matters should be faced before this important day when we start work. It is very necessary to have decided beforehand what our reactions and answers are to be in certain circumstances, rather than to be caught unprepared.

If we believe that our God has directed our steps to a particular job, then it follows that this must be the sphere in which He wishes His character to be displayed. If it was expected of slaves, "that they may adorn the doctrine of God our Saviour in all things" (Titus 2:10), how much more should it be seen in us in our easier circumstances.

In other words employment has two aspects—to earn a living and to live Christ. What a responsibility, what a privilege this! Unsaved folk are ignorant of His character and He relies on us to reveal it to them. Therefore from the very first day that we commence work we must be very careful in everything we do and say.

Our responsibility is to our employer with whom we have contracted to work. We must ensure that we fulfil our side of that contract, irrespective of whether he fulfils his side of the agreement.

We cannot serve two masters. This is an obvious fact and Scripture makes this very clear (Matt 6:24).

Whether our employer is good or bad, we are to serve to the best of our ability. Thus even slaves were enjoined to "be obedient to them that are your masters according to the flesh—in singleness of heart as unto Christ" (Eph 6:5).

Bearing this in mind we cannot contract to obey our employer and at the same time agree to obey the dictates of a union or association or guild A clear stand should be taken on this matter from the start. Not that we should act beligerently, but state clearly, simply and courteously our position as believers. However, if we are to be respected in our stand, then all other aspects of our behaviour must be consistent with our position.

We must not overlook the further point that a believer should never be in partnership with unbelievers, and such associations as trade unions clearly fall into this category. How can two walk together unless they be agreed (Amos 3:3)? Having said this it is not for us to criticise trade unions and similar associations—we are simply to keep outside them all.

In this age truth and honesty are almost unknown in the business world. It is the responsibility of all believers to make sure that these divine attributes are displayed before our fellows. No untruth or dishonest act should be countenanced. This may make us unpopular but it will be to the glory of our Lord. We must not pilfer (Titus 2:10), even though this may be the established practice of the workforce.

If we are late at work because of oversleeping, then we must say so and not pretend that the train was late. Neither should we tell others to say that we are out when someone wishes to see us—this is lying.

We will have contracted to work so many hours each week or month. We must work those hours, irrespective of what our workmates do, for not to do so is to rob our master. It is robbery just as much as taking money out of the till, and this applies whether our employer is an individual or a public body.

Sad to say in most places of employment blasphemy is prevalent. It is no good ranting about this; far better to quietly state what the Saviour means to us and how it grieves us to hear His name taken in vain.

Remember that we are paid to work, not to preach. So we are not to stop work on every possible occasion to preach to all and sundry. Nevertheless occasions will arise when clearly the opportunity has been given to us to state our beliefs, "the confession of our faith". We must make sure that we are prepared to seize such openings. Make it clear that we have a living Saviour, One who was dead but is alive and coming again.

As believers we should not gamble—would our Lord have done so?—therefore raffle tickets will be courteously declined. We will not, of course, defile our bodies, the temple of the Holy Spirit (1 Cor 6:19), by smoking. Drink may be a more subtle danger. Our workfellows will probably seek to cajole us into this by saying that there is no harm in a little. How many drunkards have started in this way! For the child of God there is no sensual stimulant and we do well to determine that we will never drink alcohol at work (or in any home). How easily we can set an example to others which will lead to their downfall through drink.

All our work is to be done neither grudgingly or reluctantly but "whatsoever ye do, do it heartily, as to the Lord and not unto men" (Col 3:23). Even the most mundane or repetitive task takes on a new importance if viewed in this way.

We are always to obey those set over us, even when we consider them to be in error. However, if their instructions are counter to divine principles and would involve us in dishonesty or untruthfulness then they must be courteously declined.

We should remember that the Lord spent His years from teenage to thirty in the carpenter's shop. We do not know the problems He experienced, but can imagine the ridicule He endured because of the principles and standards He maintained.

At the end of those years heaven was opened to attest the Father's pleasure in His life hitherto. This should be our desire, that our Father might be equally pleased with us in our work, however humdrum and far from the public eye it may be.

If we weigh these matters prayerfully and carefully, and then commit our way unto the Lord, we will find that He will help even the youngest of us day by day.

Courtship

The next milestone many of us come to is when we feel drawn to a particular member of the opposite sex and would desire to make him or her our partner for life.

Now if we are to court someone, the step must be taken very seriously. It cannot be God's will for a believer to engage in what is known as flirting, or to court one person and then another. Not only can such behaviour be emotionally harmful but it is not becoming of God's children.

The Word of God is not only to govern us in spiritual matters but is to be the ruling factor in every sphere of our lives.

Therefore we must understand clearly that it is contrary to Scripture for a believer to court an unbeliever: "What part hath he that believeth with an infidel (unbeliever)?" (2 Cor 6:15). If we are true to our confession we will be unable to have real fellowship with unbelievers, for they cannot share with us what should be the most important things in our lives.

Neither should we court a divorced person whose original partner is still living, even though he may be a believer. Marriage is for life, and cannot be broken by divorce even though the law of the land may permit it. Such a person is not free to marry in the sight of God, the original marriage being still binding.

However it is not enough that the person of our choice be a believer, we should have similar views on the authority of the Scriptures. How can we truly be at one if we break the loaf at one gathering, testifying to our oneness with that company, when our prospective partner is doing the same with believers meeting on different principles? Nor should a brother be pressurised into gathering in assembly fellowship just to obtain a partner when all the time his sympathies are elsewhere.

We must take care that our desire for a partner arises from a genuine feeling for an individual rather than from a wish to conform to the general pattern and fear of becoming the odd one out. To be single in no way marks out a person as a failure. It is clear from 1 Cor 7:30-35 that it was never the purpose of God that all should marry. As the apostle makes clear, there are areas of service where a partner is a hindrance. The unmarried are able to give their undivided attention to the things of the Lord. Paul would never have been able to give himself so completely to the service of his Lord if he had been married.

We must not chiefly be concerned with the physical attractiveness of a person; the spiritual person hidden within the physical body is more important. Neither should financial standing or prospects be the deciding factor.

Boaz sought Ruth for his partner because of her demeanour as she gleaned, and for what he had learnt of her faithfulness toward her mother-in-law, Naomi. This gives us an indication of what we should expect to see in any prospective partner.

The question naturally arises how we are to know the right partner. Like any other problem we must take the matter to our Father, asking Him, if it is His will, to prepare one to be the perfect consort for us, and, if we have a particular person in mind, to indicate to us if this has His approval. Remember the words of Abraham's servant, "I, being in the way, the Lord led me" (Gen 24:27). So we must place ourselves in His hands and be prepared to await His direction. We should never seek to force the issue ourselves. If our desires are in line with His will then He will confirm this in no uncertain way.

It is most important that these, and all other such matters, are fully talked over. In doing so we must be completely honest; it is no use hiding your true thoughts and convictions in order to avoid upsetting the one to whom you are attracted. Complete honesty is essential from the start, else disaster may come in future days, for you cannot hide these convictions for ever.

We must take care that our bodies are kept holy, pure and sanctified. The immoral standards of the present day are not to influence us to depart from the holy standards of our God. These standards were for our good, with our best interests in mind. The believer's body is "the temple of the Holy Spirit" (1 Cor 6:19) and if we are to serve in the assembly in any way the body must be presented to our God as a "holy" sacrifice (Rom 12:1). This is "the will of God, even your sanctification, that we should abstain from fornication" (1 Thess 4:3).

Never let us fall into the snare of Satan that if we company with an unbeliever we will be used of God to his salvation. While this may have been the result in some cases, in many more the believing partner has become a backslider. The teaching of 1 Cor

7:12-14 cannot be quoted to support such a step;
these verses apply where one partner has been
saved after marriage.

Right from the start we must decide what
standards are to govern our choice. The young
brother should look for one who will grow into a
real spiritual helpmeet, one who will share his
exercises and encourage him to spend time in the
study of God's Word and in the Lord's service, even
at the expense of spending time together. The
young sister should look for one who seeks to put
the things of God first and bases his decisions upon
the Word of God.

Do not be misled by the modern use of the word
love. Love is not being superficially attracted or
emotionally stirred: it is far deeper than that. Love
will desire the best for my partner, no matter what
the cost may be to myself. There is a great
difference between *like* and *love*. Love is the
thoughtful outgoing of our whole nature to
another, a willingness to sacrifice for the one loved.

Marriage

Normally the milestone of courtship leads in due course to the milestone of marriage. Although marriage is treated lightly by the world at large today, and even considered unnecessary by many, it is still of supreme importance in the mind of our God. It is an irreversible step that will change our lives in many ways and is only to be entered into in all seriousness and with due solemnity.

Marriage is to be in "the Lord" (1 Cor 7:39), which means that He must approve of every aspect of it. If this is so then our spiritual lives will mature and increase in usefulness. If this is not so, then our previous eagerness in His service may evaporate subsequently.

We must appreciate that marriage is a union for life, only broken by the death of one partner or by the coming of our Lord: "They are no more twain but one flesh; what therefore God hath joined together let not man put asunder" (Matt 18:6). "The woman which hath an husband is bound by the law to her husband so long as he liveth" (Rom 7:2). We cannot reverse this step or break the union. Divorce may be legalised by the law of the land but never by the law of God. So although a person may be divorced in the eyes of men, the marriage being terminated as far as they are concerned, yet in the eyes of God the marriage remains in being until the death of one partner.

Remember in this connection that the union of husband and wife, the closest union that we can

39

experience on earth, is a picture of the union
between Christ and the church (Eph 5:25). Dare we
suggest that this union can be broken by the
unfaithfulness of either partner?

Thus it is contrary to the command of God to
either court or marry a divorced person whose
original partner is still living. Whether the divorcee
is a believer or not is irrelevant, as is his innocence
or guilt in the case. This is a divine principle of
universal application to which there are no excep-
tions. To go through a marriage ceremony with
such does not alter the fact that in the sight of God
one would be living in adultery. Thus one should be
barred from taking one's place in fellowship with a
company of believers. For if the assembly received
such they would be condoning what is abhorrent to
a holy God. Such a person is not to be "companied
with" (1 Cor 5:11).

Again it must be emphasised that to marry an
unbeliever is clearly contrary to our Father's
expressed command, "be ye not unequally yoked
together with unbelievers" (2 Cor 6:14). (This
verse, of course, embraces every aspect of our lives,
not only marriage.)

As stated in a previous chapter never let the evil
one delude us into thinking that if we marry an
unsaved person we will be able to lead him into a
knowledge of salvation. Many believers have made
shipwreck of their spiritual and married lives by
doing this very thing. Ahab never improved
Jezebel, rather his standards were lowered to hers.

Because marriage is for life it is vital to be sure
that our prospective partner is the right one. We
must not go ahead with the marriage simply

because we have become engaged to a person. Far better to admit our error before taking the step that irrevocably binds us than to regret it for the rest of our lives.

At marriage the wife undertakes to submit to her husband, recognising that to do so reflects the relationship of the church to Christ as head and brings pleasure to Him. This is to be perfectly balanced by the husband undertaking to love his wife in the same way as Christ loved the church; that is, desiring her utmost blessing and being prepared to give his all in order to bring this about (Eph 5:22-33). It is only when each submits in this way that the perfection of marriage as purposed by God can be experienced.

This is the only basis for sustaining a marriage "in peace" (1 Cor 7:15). Each must face up to the challenge of being prepared to accept this change in position before entering into marriage. A marriage that leads to bickering and unhappiness cannot be to the glory of God.

The marriage ceremony will include certain vows for each of the two, vows to be taken in the sight of God. These must not be taken lightly, for having taken them we will be responsible to keep them for the duration of the marriage, no matter what problems may come into our lives. One partner may become permanently incapacitated and need caring for year after year. Only a properly-based marriage will stand such a strain.

It was truly said in years past that the weddings of believers were more solemn than those of unsaved folk but their funerals far more joyous. Can this be said today of the former? While a wedding is an occasion for rejoicing are we not copying the fashions of the world in the lavishness of dress and display? Is not the spiritual side taking a back place? Is it not sometimes the occasion for the foolish jesting that is so unseemly among the people of God (Eph 5:4)? Is not the use of alcoholic drink coming in, setting a bad example to others and maybe starting someone on the road to a drunkard's life? (It is no use quoting the example of the Saviour at the marriage of Cana, where non-alcoholic wine was the only drink to be had. Would the Saviour have provided the fermented grape-juice condemned in Prov 20:1?). What have believers to do with toasts? Surely the blessing of our God and Father will have been sought on the bridal pair, so how can a toast obtain a greater blessing?

To quote another, "Weddings are truly solemnised when the arrangements are such as to coincide with the mind of God and such as leave in the memory the sense of the Lord's blessing which maketh rich".

This union of husband and wife becomes operative in the sight of God as soon as the couple are pronounced man and wife. Customs and laws regarding marriage vary from country to country, but once these are complied with the two become one in the sight of God.

Marriage

(Continued)

Having obtained a partner under the guidance of our God, there will immediately arise matters for decision that will test whether or not we sincerely intend to let the Lord rule in our lives.

First of all there will be the question of the honeymoon. Is our destination to be restricted to where we can have fellowship with a company of like-minded believers? This principle should govern where we spend all our subsequent holidays and if we make an exception for our honeymoon then we are not starting our married life by putting the Lord first.

Then there is the question as to where we should live. Here again our Father has a plan for us, a street where He desires us to reveal His character. It will be situated where we can fulfil our responsibilities in a local assembly.

It is important when deciding on the actual property that we consider what claims it will make upon our time. A large garden may appear attractive but if it prevents us from serving the Lord acceptably then we should look elsewhere.

Having found the accommodation of His choice we must seek the fellowship of the nearest company of believers gathering on the basis of the New Testament, however weak and small in numbers it may be. To pass by such an assembly in order to meet with a numerically stronger one is to say in effect that the first company is not a scriptural gathering. Of course there may be errors of such a serious nature held or practised by those nearest that make it impossible to have fellowship with them. The condemnation involved in passing one assembly to go to another must be faced up to.

The house was intended to be a home, and should be where the presence of the Lord is felt, especially by the unsaved. Everything in it should be fit for His presence. There should be no books or magazines that we would not be happy to produce to Him. It should be like the home at Bethany where the Lord was free to come at any time and was happy to abide there.

It should not be kept just for ourselves but shared with the Lord's people by showing hospitality. We are only stewards of it. This does not mean putting on a *spread* but sharing what we normally have with others; not only with those who can reciprocate but even more with those who will have no opportunity of doing so. This can be a great blessing (Heb 13:2).

Consider the use made of their home by Aquila and Priscilla (Acts 18:26), who invited Apollos in order to talk over the truths of Scripture. However let us take care that hospitality is not the occasion for gossip or criticism of other believers.

Marriage is a partnership, the two becoming "one flesh" (Matt 19:6). Therefore there should be unity in purpose, in attitude and in service. One partner should never criticise the other in public, and the wife should abide by and practise the teaching of her husband.

It is the wife's responsibility to maintain the home and to care for the family; to be a "keeper at home". To quote another: "The words of Titus

2:4-5 should be sufficient deterrent to young married women abandoning their God-appointed sphere for life in the business world with a view to adding to their spending capacity. No greater tragedy can befall a home than that which promotes moral wreckage among growing children because the young mother is more concerned about material prosperity than about Christian training. Wholesale condemnation of a married woman's engagement in outside employment would be wrong, for circumstances differ, but in the main homes are happier and children better cared for and instructed, where the mother devotes herself religiously to the duties which matrimony and motherhood demand of her".

Some wives will no doubt say, "What am I to do with myself all day?" Scripture makes it clear that there is a sphere of service for young wives as well as older ones. There are those with whom we will be brought into contact who need telling of the Saviour. There are elderly believers who need practical help and above all company. It is sad when a believer in fellowship needs practical help but this is not forthcoming because all the able-bodied sisters are gainfully employed.

On the other hand it is the husband's duty to work to provide for the family. In normal circumstances one would not expect a young man to marry depending entirely upon his wife's earnings.

Husband and wife must agree as to their aims in life. Is promotion to be striven for, ignoring any effect it may have upon our availability for the Lord's service? Are we to seek a bigger house or car as soon as possible, being concerned with making a show, keeping up with others? Can this possibly be the Lord's will? Or do we agree to put Him first, trusting our Father to provide all that we have need of?

Husband and wife must both realise that they will no longer be able to do just what they please as in their single days, for each will now have to take into account the wishes of the other. This does not always come easily; it needs self-discipline on the part of both. Mistakes will be made but these must be forgiven.

Although of general application, the words of Eph 4:26 are particularly important to husbands and wives: "Let not the sun go down on your wrath". We should make sure that any differences are put right before retiring for the night.

Married couples over the passage of years should grow to be of one mind to such an extent that they will individually react to a situation in exactly the same way without any inter-communication. Remember the two on the road to Emmaus, who we believe were a married couple: "Did not our heart burn within us"—two persons, one heart. This is what marriage is all about.

Only in this way will the marriage result in a home which is a living testimony both to the power of the gospel and to an ascended Christ.

Parenthood

In the goodness of God husband and wife may be blessed with a child, thus reaching the milestone of parenthood.

Before the birth of the child both mother and father should have been prayerful that they would be given wisdom in bringing up the babe. The greatest yearning of parents must be that the child might be saved and might live to the glory of God. From birth we should determine to train the child in right paths so that the end result is an adult who will be God-honouring, God-fearing and God-pleasing, no matter what sacrifice this may necessitate on our part.

The Jews set us an example in this. They used nine specific words to describe the growth of a child from a new-born babe to a mature young man. So concerned were they that their children should be trained up to take their place among God's earthly people that the parents carefully directed the training of the child to ensure that each stage was reached, and nothing was allowed in the home that would hinder this growth.

This should be our attitude, even if problems arise as the children realise that their friends and fellow-pupils have entertainments that *they* know nothing of, and are allowed to do things forbidden to themselves.

We must realise that a child imbibes impressions from its parents far earlier in life than we normally give credit for. On the other hand the years, in the

47

will of God, during which we will be able to
influence them, will pass in a flash. There is very
little time, in fact, in which to train up a child in the
nurture and admonition of the Lord, and we cannot
afford to waste any of it. There will come a day
when our children will launch out into the world
and we will have to rest then on what we have
taught them in the past.

Another has said, "Childhood is the most
impressionable period of life. Every object soon
becomes a book; every place a schoolhouse; every
event ploughs in some seed which will bear its
appropriate fruit for years to come. The characters
graven in the tender bark grow larger with the
advancing age of the tree. Parents, in their Bible
teaching, should seize upon these golden hours. If
they delay to cast the good seed into the virgin soil,
the enemy will sow his tares and occupy the
ground".

God has entrusted each little life to us to bring up
for Him, not for ourselves: "Take this child and
nurse it for me" (Exod 2:9). We will never have a
more precious object in our care. What we do can
affect the child's attitude to the gospel in later
years. If we are aware of this we will be careful
what we bring into the home, allowing only what
will influence the child for good.

The child must be disciplined and taught to obey.
This does not imply harshness or severity; but an
undisciplined child grows up into an undisciplined
adult, causing trouble both in the assembly and in
the world. Remember the awful warning of
Adonijah, whose father David "had not displeased
him at any time" (1 Kings 1:6).

Fill the child's mind as early as possible with Bible stories. These will bring out in a simple way the plan of salvation, but one should never put pressure on a child to make a profession of salvation. On the other hand we should never express scepticism when such a profession is made, even if we have some doubt as to its reality.

The mother will have the most influence on the child. This is clearly why the Old Testament gives the names of so many mothers, linking them with the good or bad characters of their sons. The apostle links the faith of Timothy with the teaching of his mother and grandmother (2 Tim 3:15).

The child should be taught that the Lord's Day is to be reserved for the Lord; only those duties that are necessary are performed. This is not a matter of legality but of giving Him that which we are free to do in this country. Parents should not listen to the news or buy a newspaper on that day. Nowadays believers seem happy to travel on the Lord's Day as a matter of convenience or for the purpose of holidays. Can we wonder that the unsaved have lost all respect for that day?

We must set an example in all that we say and do. A child will be quick to notice any inconsistency between our life in the home and in the assembly. Truthfulness should characterise us at all times, for our children will take their standards from our example. If we cannot answer their questions then we must say so and not give an untrue reply.

It should be evident to the child that the assembly is very precious to us, as it is to God, "bought with the blood of His Own" (Acts 20:28). Never let us criticise the assembly or individual believers in

front of the family or find fault with those who
have occupied the platform.

From earliest days children should be taken to the
Lord's Supper, and taught to sit quietly, not
distracting others. The truths concerning the
Saviour and His work that are imbibed unconsciously
at such times will never be erased from their minds.

In our desire to train our children aright there is
the danger of continually nagging them, constantly
finding fault. This may cause them to give up trying
to please us, feeling that it is an impossible task.
This is why it is written, "Fathers provoke not your
children to anger lest they be discouraged" (Col
3:21).

We must appreciate that just as marriage
brought a complete change in our lives and
relationships, so the coming of an infant will bring
another radical change. No longer will the wife be
able to devote all her attentions to her husband. No
longer will they be able to go out together
whenever they wish. The oneness of husband and
wife will be tested by sleepless nights and exhausting
days.

May the priority in life of each parent be that
their child may, like Samuel, "grow before the
Lord", grow on and be "in favour...with the Lord",
and "minister unto the Lord".

Miscellaneous

We have now considered ten important milestones which arise during the lives of most believers.

However life is full of milestones, testing times or new experiences that mark stageposts in our lives. We come to fresh circumstances, maybe of joy or of tragedy; maybe in the family or in the assembly; maybe at college or at work. Almost without exception these events come upon us with little or no warning. How can we prepare ourselves for such, not knowing from day to day what lies ahead?

The Scriptures have been given to meet our need in this respect, containing many examples of such situations. The more we assimilate these the more prepared we shall be to react in the right way when such events occur.

The first of these appears in Gen 3, when Eve had to decide whether or not she would trust God and submit to His command. Such a test will surely come our way at some time, and, like her, it will be easy to find excuses for disobeying. If we do this we will inevitably lose the blessing that would have been ours, and others may suffer as a consequence. How essential to have hidden His Word in our hearts beforehand, being assured of its certainty and that it was given for our good.

Then there is Noah; instructed to build an ark when he had never known rain, yet obeyed because it was God's command. Maybe such a situation will face us, when His will appears to be ridiculous by

human reasoning. It is imperative for His glory that
we obey. The disciples were placed in the same
position with regard to the miraculous draught of
fishes (John 21:6).

Believers must inevitably face the decision
whether to be separated from this world system
with all its attractions and seeming prosperity.
Abraham is our example here, Lot the solemn
warning (Gen 13). The brevity of this world's
material wealth is seen in the destruction of Sodom
and Gomorrah. Abraham's separation from all such
is clearly vindicated by the subsequent history.

The children of Israel were faced with a series of
milestones on their journey from Egypt to Canaan:
the sudden coming upon the Red Sea; the appearing
of the Egyptian army in the rear; no water or food;
the attack of Amalek; the Satanic suggestion of the
golden calf. These are but a selection; let us
consider them individually.

At some time we will be confronted with a
sudden impasse—a situation from which there
appears to be no escape. The word comes as clearly
to us as to Israel, "Fear not, stand still and see the
salvation of the Lord" (Exod 14:33). To base our
actions on common sense in such circumstances is
to court disaster. Yet when there comes a clear
command to act in a certain way we must not
hesitate, but go forward in faith, however impossible
it may seem.

There will also be occasions when the forces
opposed to us will appear to have us at their mercy.
Conscious of our weakness and inability to deliver
ourselves, we must listen to the divine voice, "The
Lord shall fight for you" (Exod 14:14).

Then there will be times of great disappointment, all our expectations coming to nothing—not obtaining the job which we thought was certain; the house we were purchasing suddenly becoming not available—the list is endless. This is what Israel experienced when they arrived at Marah (Exod 15:23). Expecting refreshment they found bitterness. Yet this was intended to teach them to trust Jehovah in a deeper way than hitherto, and the same applies to us. That is why it was a tree, speaking of the cross, that was thrown into the waters to make them drinkable: "Who passing through the valley of Baca (weeping) make it a well" (Psa 84:6).

Probably we will not have been saved very long before we will find the evil one, the enemy of souls, attacking us. Amalek is a picture of this and the enemy is the flesh, that old nature of ours that can still respond to the temptations of Satan, who attacks subtly and not openly. Those who are not growing spiritually, "the hindmost...all that were feeble" (Deut 25:18), are particularly susceptible to his onsets. The remedy is not in ourselves but in prayer—the prayer of faith in the delivering power of a risen Christ—pictured in the rod of deliverance held up before Jehovah.

Sooner or later we will be placed under great pressure to do what it contrary to Scripture, as Aaron was in the making of the golden calf. Others, maybe even professing Christians, will try to force us to do this. We must follow the example of the Levites and maintain the honour of our God even at the expense of separating ourselves from our relatives and friends.

Then there is the milestone of being wrongly accused, as Aaron and Moses were on more than one occasion; they said nothing in self-justification but "returned unto the Lord" and told Him all about it. Nearly forty years later, in similar circumstances (Exod 20:6), their response was to go to the door of the tabernacle and fall upon their faces before Him.

When they arrived at the land of Gilead Israel had reached another milestone (Num 32). Were they to be satisfied with the attractive pasture land around them, or were they to go on to the land "flowing with milk and honey" which Jehovah had prepared for them? Two and a half tribes failed this test, and settled down outside Canaan. They knew nothing of worship in the place where God was to put His name, and were the first to be carried into captivity. This is a simple picture of the choice facing believers—are we to be satisfied with being saved, but never taking our place with Christ as dead to the world and as a result miss the spiritual blessings that He saved us to enjoy?

Isaiah reached a milestone in his life when the call to service came. It will definitely come to us, but will our response be the same, "Here am I, send me" (Isa 6:8)? Such a servant must be ready when called, and willing to be a sanctified channel through whom the Lord can speak and act.

Job's experiences are recorded to prepare us for the milestone of tragedy and suffering. His trials were probably more severe than any we shall be called to pass through. Yet he worshipped and did not doubt God. He knew it was a refining process that would result in his coming forth as gold (Job 23:10).

These are but a few examples. We have left out David, faced with the challenge of Goliath. Hezekiah threatened in the letter from the Assyrian, Daniel being offered food not fit for God's people, and many more. These contain all the instruction necessary to prepare us for whatever milestones we may come to in our way.

By careful reading of the Scriptures with this in mind we shall be thoroughly equipped for every circumstance of life.

Questions
Young People Ask

by David Newell

Can I Trust The Bible?

"Of course, I believe in the Lord Jesus as my Saviour, but I just can't accept everything I read in the Bible."

This sentiment is often expressed by young Christians influenced by a worldly outlook which dismisses much, if not all, of God's Word as "unscientific", "mythical", and "obsolete". Despite its apparently high view of the Lord Jesus, this kind of remark conceals a basic fallacy, and that is that we can implicitly trust the Saviour but not the Scriptures.

Let me suggest two reasons why this is fundamentally wrong. First, Christ and the Bible are ultimately inseparable in that both bear the same grand title of "the Word" (John 1:1; 1 Pet 1:25). They give testimony to each other, and the Saviour is Himself the climax of God's message spoken to man (Heb 1:1, 2). Second, as far as the believer is concerned, the greatest single evidence for the trustworthiness of Scripture is the teaching of Christ. After all, a Christian is one who has submitted himself unreservedly to a Saviour who claims emphatically to be "the Truth" (John 14:6), and insists that those owning His Lordship demonstrate it in absolute obedience (Luke 6:46). Therefore, to honour the Lord Jesus we *must* accept His view of Scripture. There is no alternative for the consistent Christian.

What, then, did the Master teach? We can summarise it in three words:

1. authority,
2. inerrancy,
3. sufficiency.

In John 10:34-36, the Lord defends His claims to deity by reference to the Old Testament, bringing together these three important truths for our instruction: "Jesus answered them, Is it not written in your law, I said, Ye are gods? If he called them gods, unto whom the word of God came, and the scripture cannot be broken; Say ye of him, whom the Father hath sanctified, and sent into the world, Thou blasphemest; because I said, I am the Son of God?"

1. Authority. In calling the Old Testament "the word of God" (v. 35), the Lord Jesus is simply underlining its supernatural origin. Of course, God used human instruments to pen His words, but it is still His voice that we hear speaking. The constant "Thus saith the Lord" of the prophets is no barren formula: it is a weighty and necessary reminder that we are listening, not to human reasoning, but to divine revelation.

At Pentecost, Peter carefully distinguishes between the message and the mouthpiece: "This scripture must needs have been fulfilled, which the Holy Spirit by the mouth of David spake" (Acts 1:16). How reverently we should approach a Book which is in its entirety the counsel of the living God! Writes the Psalmist: "Bless the Lord, ye his angels, that excel in strength, that do his commandments, hearkening unto the voice of his Word" (Psa 103:20). In our daily Bible reading, do we grasp the astounding truth that this is God's voice, as real, as powerful, as authoritative as if He had spoken audibly from heaven? May we be like the Thessalonians who received the gospel "not as the word of men, but as it is in truth, the word of God" (1 Thess 2:13).

2. Inerrancy. If *authority* emphasises the power of the Word, *inerrancy* highlights its purity, "free from all falsehood or mistake...[and] entirely true and trustworthy in all its assertions".[1] This is what the Lord Jesus is teaching when He maintains that "the scripture cannot be broken" (v.35). Over 60 times He quotes from the Old Testament (and from no other source), never to criticise but always to confirm its accuracy. Consider some of the specific historical events He corroborates: the creation account (Matt 19:4, 5), the first murder (Luke 11:51), the universal flood (Matt 24:37-39), the destruction of Sodom (Luke 17:29). We cannot escape the fact that the Saviour gave His stamp of approval to the Old Testament as God's inspired and flawless Word. Indeed, He goes so far as to ask how people can believe Him if they reject the words of Moses (John 5:46, 47)! It is logically impossible for one who accepts the authority of Christ to doubt any part of the Old Testament.

3. Sufficiency. The authoritative, inerrant Bible is no dry, dusty text-book; rather, it is gloriously sufficient to meet the believer's every need. The Lord Jesus takes the Old Testament as His ultimate court of appeal when answering the Jews: "Is it not written in your law?" (v.34). Thus, when problems, questions, and storms arise, we must turn to the Book.

The sufficiency of Scripture is superbly illustrated in the way the Lord Jesus defeats Satan in the desert. The old serpent is put to flight by the simple but effective quotation of appropriate Scriptures (Matt 4:4, 7, 10). The child of God requires not a university education but a thorough knowledge of the Bible to conquer the doubts and fears with which Satan seeks to corrupt our minds. But remember! In order to use this sharpest of two-edged swords we must get to know it well. It is only the devoted student of the Word who will truly prove its sufficiency in time of need.

Lest any object that the Lord Jesus is validating only the Old Testament, we can show that He also authenticates the New in advance. "The Holy Spirit...shall...bring all things to your remembrance, whatsoever I have said unto you" (John 14:26). These words anticipate and pre-authenticate the Gospels. "He will guide you into all truth" and "He will show you things to come" (John 16:13) cover the letters and the Revelation. These writings too are authoritative, inerrant, and sufficient, for they derive from the Spirit who reveals all necessary truth. The New Testament writers themselves recognised that they were penning God's Word (1 Cor 14:37), and could thus place their books on a level with the Old Testament (2 Pet 3:2, 16).

The conclusion is plain. If we trust the Lord Jesus we must trust the whole Bible, for it bears His seal of approval. Let us then turn from the error of our opening quotation to the godly example of Handley Moule who said, "I am going, not in a blind sense, but reverently, to trust the Book because of *Him*".[2]

References:

1. "The Chicago Statement on Biblical Inerrancy 1978", cited in John F. MacArthur Jr., *Why Believe the Bible,* Gospel Light, 1980, p.18.

2. Quoted in R. Pache, *The Inspiration and Authority of Scripture,* Moody Press, 1969, p. 223.

How Should I Study The Bible?

Our God is economical with miracles. Having made man in His image (Gen 1:27), having provided a perfect instruction book through supernatural inspiration (2 Pet 1:21), and having given us the best of all teachers in the Holy Spirit (John 16:13), He will work no fourth miracle to transfer truth from the Scriptures into our minds. In other words, there is no short-cut to spirituality! Only through the solid and systematic study of God's Word will the young believer grow in the knowledge of God, and thus be able to stand firm against the storms of the world, the flesh, and the devil. And that means hard work.

The Bereans in Acts 17:11, 12 provide a pattern. They studied the Scriptures purposefully ("searched"), eagerly ("with all readiness of mind"), regularly ("daily"), and fruitfully ("therefore many of them believed"). No suggestion here that they found time occupied with the Word tedious or ill-spent! If we come to God's Book with humble expectancy we shall never be disappointed, but, like the Psalmist, "rejoice at thy word, as one that findeth great spoil" (Psa 119:162). Of course, if we are determined to be bored, we shall be, for "as [a man] thinketh in his heart, so is he" (Prov 23:7). But there is no need. What can be more thrilling than to engage our minds with the infallible truth of the living God? What can be more relevant? To live joyfully in God's world we must live by God's Word.

How then can the young Christian study his

Bible? Here are some sugestions.

Aids to Study. The simplest aids are the best.
Instead of recommending a multitude of commen-
taries, let us just list those tools with which any
believer can dig out the treasures of God's Word.
First, a good standard Bible is required. The A.V. is
as good as any (and considerably better than most)
for close study. By all means consult other versions,
but always stick to one reliable translation as your
basic text. Second, obtain a notebook and pen,
because it is important to record what the Lord
teaches you for future encouragement. Moses sets
the example in Exod 17:14, interestingly the first
mention of writing in Scripture. Third, a concordance
is essential, and Young's is probably the easiest to
use. With that you can trace the meaning of
significant Bible words, for Scripture is always its
own best interpreter. And don't neglect those
marginal references in your Bible. They will often
direct you to parallel passages and related verses.

All this, naturally, takes time. But is is time well
spent (Eph 5:16). Real Bible study, you see, is costly.
To the young man who said, "I'd give the world to
understand the Bible as you do", Harold St. John
replied, "That's exactly what it cost me".

Approaches to Study. The discovery of the empty
tomb in John 20 illustrates the ideal approach to
Scripture. In verses 5 to 8 the verb "to see" occurs
three times in the A.V., but actually represents
three different Greek words. These suggest the key
steps in Bible study.

1. Confrontation (v.5). The word "saw" here
simply means "to notice". John had to stoop and
enter the tomb to notice its contents. And we must
submissively open up God's Word if its life-
transforming truth is to have any impact. Make the
Psalmist's prayer your own: "Open thou mine eyes,
that I may behold wondrous things out of thy law"
(Psa 119:18). Consecutive reading from Genesis to
Revelation is indispensible—and don't omit the
difficult passages! To get to grips with a particular
book, keep reading and re-reading until your mind
is saturated with it. There can be no substitute for
the Bible itself. The ready availability of so much
Christian literature today lures us into reading
books about Scripture instead of Scripture itself.
Deut 11:18-21 is a challenging reminder of the
place the undiluted Word of God should have in our
lives.

2. Observation (vv.6, 7). "Seeth" here means "to
see, noting details". Peter observes the arrangement
of the burial clothes within the tomb. That
demands more than a passing glance. To get the
most from Scripture, we must read thoughtfully
and seriously—and *slowly*. God will *not* reveal His
will to those who treat His Word with careless
haste.

Serious study involves "rightly dividing the word
of truth" (2 Tim 2:15), which means, among other
things, due regard for *context* (for example, the
context of those favourite verses Phil 4:7 and 19),
common sense (identifying figurative language in, say,
Matt 23:14), and *comparison* (many a difficult verse is
explained by a related passage). Observe carefully:

this Book demands *total concentration*.

3. Interpretation (v.8). "Saw" signifies "to discern"; that is, to work out the meaning of what is seen. John rightly interprets the orderly placing of those clothes as evidence for the Lord's resurrection. And when we read the Word, we must be on the alert for the correct meaning. A grasp of the overall purpose and structure of each book will guard us against a good many errors of interpretation.

4. Application (v.8). John believes what he sees. All Scripture is to be trusted and, as it concerns us, obeyed. Indeed, the very reading of it will strengthen our faith (Rom 10:17). Says Bengel, "Apply thyself wholly to the Scriptures, and apply the Scriptures wholly to thyself". Ultimately, the aim of Bible study is not to feed our curiosity but to mould our lives for God. Like New Testament prophecy it is for "edification [doctrine, for the head], exhortation [duty, for the hands], and comfort [devotion, for the heart]" (1 Cor 14:3). Is my study of the Word having a real influence in my life? If it is not, something is fundamentally amiss.

The time is short. Let us reassess our priorities and invest our time, talents and energy in the serious study of God's Word. After all, only this will count for eternity.

Why Do I Need Fellowship?

Young Christians sometimes query why so much is made of assembly fellowship. Now, it is good to ask questions—as long as we recognise that the God who made and saved us alone knows what is best for us. In other words, our questions can be answered only as we submit to the Scriptures of Truth.

Man's basic need for fellowship stems from his creation, for God said of Adam, "It is not good that the man should be alone" (Gen 2:18). We are so made that we crave the benefits of human companionship (Eccles 4:9-12). And when saved by grace, we find a new need for the company of God's people. It is noteworthy that the disciples were called into a group (Mark 3:13, 14) which the Saviour trained, protected and commissioned to bear His message (Matt 28:18-20). Significant, too, is the high proportion of New Testament letters addressed, not to individuals, but to assemblies. You see, our God specialises in *togetherness*. Having rescued sinners through the precious blood of His Son, He places them instantaneously in the glorious company of the redeemed, the Body of Christ (1 Cor 12:13). This is simple fact. But He also expects and indeed commands them to associate together in companies normally known as local churches or assemblies. Matt 18:17-20, Acts 2:41, 42, and Heb 10:25 all assume the existence of a recognisable gathering of believers, meeting regularly for mutual blessing, in obedience to the Word.

What I am emphasising is that the Biblical concept of fellowship cannot be divorced from the truth of the local assembly. In a world where new "Christian" organisations, societies, and missions spring up overnight, it has to be repeated firmly that the Scriptural setting for all spiritual activity and growth is the local church. God's Word knows nothing else. Therefore, whatever may be urged in favour of, say, a college Christian Union, or the Gideons (and we praise God for His blessing through such endeavours), our first priority *must* be the assembly.

But what does fellowship mean? I have a suspicion that many of us use Biblical words without real understanding, so let us define our term. It means "sharing", or "participation". "Partnership" renders it particularly well, shifting the emphasis from enjoyable privilege, which most people (quite rightly) associate with fellowship, to solemn responsibility, an aspect all too often overlooked. Being a Christian involves a serious duty both towards the Lord (1 Cor 1:9) and the Lord's people (2 Cor 8:4).

Remembering, then, that the word implies partnership, that it is essential for all believers, and that it is inextricably linked with the local assembly, what does it involve?

1. Work. If I am in a partnership, I cannot afford to sit back and do nothing. I must work! In Phil 4:3, Paul underlines the effort involved in genuine commitment to an assembly. He speaks gratefully of a "true yokefellow", and of two women who have "laboured with me [shared my struggle, N.A.S.B.]

in the gospel" as "fellowlabourers". All energetic
words, these! Both men and women are called upon
to involve themselves sacrificially, faithfully and
unceasingly in the work of the Lord's assembly.
Perhaps we had better ask ourselves how valuable
our contribution is to the church in which God has
placed us. Are we building up or knocking down?
May it be said of us, "the people had a mind to work"
(Neh 4:6).

2. Warmth. How comforting is a warm fire on a
cold day! Fellowship is equally cheering, for how
would we ever keep going without the loving
encouragement of our brothers and sisters? Many
of us can testify to the value of consistent assembly
fellowship as a tonic for our weakness, and a
corrective for our errors. The hallmark of the early
saints was mutual love (John 13:35), and it certainly
showed in the first assemblies (Phil 1:9; Col 1:4). Of
course, to enjoy this glowing experience, we have
to be regularly with our brethren. Are *you* keeping
warm?

3. Worship. The Father seeks worshippers (John
4:23), and one of the grand privileges of being saved
is that we are able to praise the God who has done
so much for us. Although we can, and should, spend
time in personal adoration of the Lord, both the Old
and New Testaments indicate the special value of
corporate worship. Thus the Troas disciples gathered
on the first day of the week, *not* primarily to hear
Paul, but "to break bread" in memory of the Saviour
(Acts 20:7). Without endorsing the practice of
referring to it as the "Worship Meeting" (for *all*

Christian gatherings involve worship), we must acknowledge that this simple remembrance of the Master is the believer's highest occupation.

4. Witness. New Testament evangelism is always designed to establish or build up an assembly. That is one reason why some of us are a little distrustful of mass crusades. Their existence is a sad testimony to our failure in gospel work. But the local church should always be a centre for evangelistic outreach. Some find it hard to speak up well for the Lord, but as a company we can support one another and enjoy the thrill of "fellowship in the gospel" (Phil 1:5). Once we lose that we have lost all.

5. Warfare. The young Christian soon discovers that he is not involved in a casual game, but in a strenuous conflict against spiritual foes (Eph 6:12). To do battle against Satan, every Christian soldier needs all the back-up he can get. After the apostles had been threatened by the Jewish authorities, they returned to "their own company" (Acts 4:23) to join in fervent prayer for boldness to continue in the truth. You see, the best remedy for fear or defeat is the Prayer Meeting, where the Lord's people close ranks to protect their own and put to flight the enemy.

We all desperately need our local assembly; and it needs us. Someone has said, alluding to Matt 18:20, that the most faithful attender of assembly meetings is the Lord Jesus. Doesn't it make good sense, then, for us to be there too?

How Can I Learn To Pray?

A little while ago, a Christian young lady confessed to me that she was having difficulty with her personal prayer life. I cannot quite remember my exact reply, but it certainly should have included the phrase, "So am I"! Something the believer learns as he grows in grace is that the really tough issues of the Christian life are the basics—prayer, Bible study, fellowship, and witness. I find all of those hard, and I am more and more convinced from Scripture that they will *never* become easy. But with the aid of the Holy Spirit we can keep on "continuing steadfastly" despite everything.

One of the great men of the Old Testament provides a challenging example of the simple conditions for effective prayer. In Gen 18 we read about Abraham's intercession on behalf of Sodom (vv. 23-32), and we can draw four lessons from that narrative.

1. Abraham Attended to the Lord (vv. 9-21). It is frequently forgotten that Abraham's prayer at the end of the chapter is no spontaneous outburst. Rather, it is the considered result of what he has learned through listening to the Lord. If you check the entire Genesis account of his life, you will find, perhaps to your surprise, that God talks to Abraham about three times as much as Abraham talks to God. There is a simple point here. If we want to speak to the Lord, we must first of all listen to Him. Prayer and Bible reading are inseparable.

Many of our nervous "if it be Thy will" prayers could be converted into definite, faithful petitions if only we took the trouble to seek the will of God as revealed in Scripture.

What did Abraham learn from God in the first part of the chapter? He learned that God longs to bless His people (vv. 10-14), and our God is still the same. The Lord Jesus ascended back to glory in an attitude of blessing (Luke 24:51), and that has ever characterised His dealings with His saints (Eph 1:3). Such knowledge should encourage us to spend much time with a God whose desire is for our good!

Second, he learned that God is the God of judgment (vv. 17-21). Much contemporary gospel preaching has diluted the clear New Testament message of salvation in Christ by omitting or soft-pedalling the truth of judgment. But be sure of this! Our God *will* judge (see especially Rom 2:1-16)— and just as this news impelled Abraham to intercede for his backsliding nephew Lot, so should it force us to our knees on behalf of unsaved friends and worldly brethren.

Third, Abraham was reminded of divine omnipotence (v. 14). This glorious truth, repeated in Luke 1:37, is the backbone of prayer, for the God of the Bible is all-powerful, and therefore "able to do exceedingly abundantly above all that we ask or think" (Eph 3:20).

Fourth, he witnessed a stunning demonstration of God's omniscience: the Lord knew Sarah's thoughts (vv. 10-13)! There are times when the believer can hardly put his prayer into words, but (and here's the comfort) our heavenly Father *knows* all about us (Matt 6:8), and the indwelling Spirit speaks up for us (Rom 8:26, 27).

If you read Genesis 18 thoroughly, you will find
that Abraham also learned about God's love to
confide in his friends (v. 17), His plans for the
patriarch's descendants (v. 18), and His faithfulness
to His Word (v. 19). Can I suggest that our prayers
will only be as full and effectual as our appreciation
of Scripture? If our prayers are Bible-based, then
we shall pray according to His will. As one has said,
"Prayer is a mighty instrument, not for getting
man's will done in heaven, but for getting God's will
done on earth".

2. Abraham Approached the Lord (v. 23). Now it is
possible to have a fine knowledge of Scripture and
still not pray. Abraham, however, was a practical
believer. What the Lord taught him he put into
immediate practice, and "drew near".

You will notice that the two angels have gone (v.
22), and God and His child are alone. The Lord Jesus
underlined the value of this in Matt 6:6: "when
thou prayest, enter into thy closet [inner room]
and when thou hast shut thy door, pray..." Do not
forget: shut that door! The world and the devil are
quick to use any distraction to hinder our communion
with the Lord. It is therefore vital to make a
deliberate effort to be

"Shut in with Thee, far, far above
The restless world that wars below."

And, wonderful to relate, as we approach God, He
approaches us (Jas 4:8).

3. Abraham Asked the Lord (vv. 23-32). That is
what prayer is all about—speaking to God. Abraham

had no time to go to a special place (after all, the Lord was there), or get himself into the right mood, or wait until he felt led to pray. He just prayed! Did not the Master say "Ask, and it shall be given you" (Luke 11:9)? How foolish we are, then, to worry and fret and fumble instead of humbly speaking to Him!

The prayer itself is *simple, sincere, short* (the Bible does *not* put a premium on long-windedness, although some of our brethren seem to!), *sensible,* in that it is in keeping with Abraham's knowledge of God, and *specific,* for it gets straight to the point. Abraham prayed on the basis of what he knew about God. Believers today possess a much fuller revelation, because we have the Lord Jesus, God's last word to man (Heb 1:1, 2). Thus we can associate our prayers with the precious name of Christ (John 16:23).

My mother taught me, as a little boy, always to end my prayers with "in the name of the Lord Jesus, Amen". When I asked why I had to say this, she replied, "Because God loves to hear it". And I cannot think of a better theological answer! The name of God's beloved Son means so much in heaven, that the Father is overjoyed to receive and answer the prayers of all who take it reverently on their lips.

4. Abraham Anticipated an Answer (19:27-29). Here is the evidence that Abraham prayed in faith (Matt 21:22). He rose up early and returned to the spot where he had spoken with the Lord. Now, God did *not* grant his specific request, because there just were not ten righteous people in Sodom (Gen

19:15). But God still satisfied the desire of Abraham's heart, that his nephew should be spared, by taking Lot out of the city before judgment fell (Gen 19:16). The answer, not exactly what Abraham expected, was perfect! You see, God reserves the right to give us His very best.

"God remembered Abraham" (Gen 19:29, and compare v. 22). What a testimony to the value of his prayers! We today are just as needy as ever Abraham was, and our God is just as gracious. So do not miss out on the privilege of regularly talking with the heavenly Father.

How is *your* prayer life getting on?

What About The Holy Spirit?

It is a tragic thing that the Holy Spirit is the most misunderstood and misrepresented Person of the Godhead today. And yet He is also probably the most talked about! His name is glibly associated with a whole host of dubious teachings and practices, many of which appear to display little of that holiness which is His characteristic quality.

In the following chapter we shall attempt to come to some Biblical conclusions about the nature of the modern charismatic movement, but we must first lay a solid Scriptural foundation for our overall understanding of the Spirit's work today. Such a foundation is provided by the Lord Jesus Himself in John 16. Here we find four principles governing the ministry of the Holy Spirit.

1. The Principle of Glorification. Says the Saviour, "He [the Holy Spirit] shall glorify Me: for He shall receive of Mine, and shall show it unto you" (John 16:14). Notice: the grand goal of the Spirit's work is to exalt *not* Himself but the Son of God. His is a self-effacing ministry, for He casts the spotlight away from Himself onto the Saviour. We find Him doing just that in Acts 5:29-32, where Peter cites Him as a witness to the Lord's exaltation: "And we are His witnesses of these things; and so is also the Holy Spirit..." Likewise, Paul asserts in 1 Cor 12:3 that it is impossible for men genuinely to own Christ's Lordship in life and language save by the Spirit.

When, therefore, we observe that specific allusions
to the Holy Spirit decrease as the Book of the Acts
progresses, this is evidence, not of failure, but of
His unqualified success in focussing on the Lord
Jesus as the Object of faith (Acts 4:12; 28:31).
Further, the principle of glorification provides a
touchstone for all the teaching we hear, because
any system of doctrine which does not exalt the
Lord Jesus is not of the Holy Spirit. This should
guard us against the modern preoccupation with
the Spirit Himself, or with the gifts rather than the
Giver. Remember: the Holy Spirit always delights
to join with the Father in directing our gaze
towards the Son (Matt 3:16-17).

2. The Principle of Harmonisation. You will have
noticed that the Lord Jesus chooses to underline the
absolute reliability of the Spirit's testimony by
three times calling Him the Spirit of Truth (John
14:17; 15:26; 16:13). As He is truth, so, in its
entirety, is the Word He inspires (2 Pet 1:21; John
17:17).

It follows logically that the Spirit of God, so
intimately involved in the *inspiration* of Scripture,
will Himself be characterised in His operations
today by a total *harmonisation* with Scripture. He
cannot contradict Himself. Here is another valuable
test for the believer: the Spirit will *never* lead us
contrary to the Word. You see, it is all too easy to
claim spiritual guidance. Even real Christians can
mistake their own inclinations for a divine impulse,
for we still possess an old nature and a heart that is
"deceitful above all things" (Jer 17:9). But we also
have a perfect standard of truth against which to

judge our feelings and experiences, and that is the
Spirit-inspired, infallible, objective Word. On this
basis, we can say that (for example) the Holy Spirit
will never lead a believer to date an unbeliever (see
2 Cor 6:14), or prompt a Christian woman to pray
publicly in an assembly meeting (see 1 Cor 14:34).
Such things may happen—but they are categorically
not the work of the Spirit!

How much, then, we need to be ruled by the
Word, for we shall only be consciously led of the
Spirit in so far as we know our Bibles. There is, alas,
no short-cut to godliness! The men God uses are
men immersed in the Scripture, and that involves
effort. To be people of the Spirit we must be people
of the Book.

3. The Principle of Education. "He will guide you
into all truth" (John 16:13) is not merely the Lord's
pre-authentication of the New Testament; it
anticipates the Spirit's activity as an instructor in
divine things. As Paul teaches, only through the
Spirit of God can divine truths be appreciated (1
Cor 2:11-14). While *inspiration* refers to His super-
intendence of the writing of Scripture, *illumination*
describes His continuing ministry in expounding it
to us.

The importance of this is seen in the Saviour's
remark that "It is expedient [better] for you that I
go away" (John 16:7). Better that the disciples'
Teacher, Guide and Counsellor should leave them?
Yes, because the Lord would then send "another
Comforter", just like Himself, to stay with them for
ever (John 14:16) and complete their spiritual
education. At Pentecost that Comforter descended,

and has ever since taken up permanent residence in the believer's heart at the moment of conversion, so that we are instantaneously *born, baptised, indwelt,* and *sealed* by the Spirit (John 3:5; 1 Cor 12:13; 1 Cor 6:19; Eph 1:13). Notice, please, that *every Christian* possesses the indwelling Spirit of God, for "if any man have not the Spirit of Christ, he is none of his" (Rom 8:9). And His desire is to lead us to "put to death the deeds of the body" (Rom 8:13, Newberry), and to display His Christ-like fruit in our lives (Gal 5:22-24).

These manifestations of the Spirit are more telling (and more costly) than all the sign gifts in the world!

4. The Principle of Application. "He shall take of mine, and shall show it unto you" (John 16:15). The story of Abraham's dedicated servant seeking a bride for Isaac is a delightful picture of this aspect of the Spirit's work. Just as he presented Rebekah with tokens of her future husband's wealth and glory (Gen 24:53), so the Holy Spirit takes the riches of Christ Jesus and makes them real to us. No wonder Paul calls Him "the earnest [or, foretaste] of our inheritance" (Eph 1:14).

Why is it, when we gather to remember the Lord as He requested, that our hearts are drawn to the greatness of His person and work? Why is it that all believers long earnestly for the Saviour's return? Why is it that the Scriptures are an inexhaustible storehouse of thrilling divine truths? Because the Spirit of God is doing His work! As one has written, "the great thrust of His combined ministries is *to keep the believer satisfied with Christ"!*[1] If we enshrine that thought at the heart of our doctrine of the Holy Spirit, we shall not go astray.

Reference:
1. R. T. Ketcham, *God's Provision for Normal Christian Living*, Moody Press, 1960, p. 141.

How Should I View
The Charismatic Movement?

This century has seen the startling development of a movement among Christians which has overflowed traditional denominational boundaries and fast promises to become a major prop of ecumenism. How should the young believer respond to the amazing claims and undeniably attractive appeal of the charismatic movement, with its offers of instant spiritual success, with supernatural experiences, and the revival of New Testament miracles?

Let me first explain the meaning of that much abused word "charismatic". It comes from a Greek word signifying "a gift involving grace (*charis*) on the part of God as the donor"[1]. In the Scriptural sense, then, every believer is charismatic in that he is, first, a recipient of God's gracious gift of salvation (Rom 5:15, 16; 6:23); and second, in posession of at least one gift of service for the benefit of the assembly (Rom 12:6).

Here now are four reasons why I reject the distinctive claims and practices of the modern charismatic movement.

1. It Misunderstands the Purpose of Bible Miracles.
One of the first things to say about miracles in the Bible is that they are infrequent. They occur in clusters at certain crucial moments in redemptive history, usually to mark some new stage in the divine dealings with man—at the exodus from Egypt, during the time of Elijah and Elisha, during

the ministry of the Saviour and His apostles. But great stretches of Bible history are bare of miracles in the specific sense of sensational divine wonders. Consider the godly men who worked no miracles at all: Abraham, David, Jeremiah, Daniel, John Baptist —and the last of these was the greatest mere man who has ever lived (Matt 11:11).

Our conclusion must be that miracles depend ultimately not on the faith or spirituality of the worker but on the purposes of God. No believer denies that our God is able to do today what He did in the past, for He is unchanging (Mal 3:6). The crucial question is, what is His will today? The New Testament indicates: 1. that miracles are *signs* identifying a messenger from God (Luke 11:20; John 5:36; John 10:24-26); 2. that the Jews particularly looked for signs (1 Cor 1:22); 3. that the signs authenticated the Lord Jesus and His apostles (Acts 2:22; 5:12; 2 Cor 12:12; Heb 2:2-4).

Since the apostles laid the foundation of the Church (Eph 2:20), and since there are no more apostles today (Rev 21:14), those identifying credentials have passed away. The believer now rests on the complete Word of God given through the apostles (2 Pet 3:2), not on sign miracles. And how infinitely more glorifying it is to God that His people should simply trust Him, instead of seeking the sensational and spectacular!

2. It Devalues Miracles. This may seem an astonishing criticism of a movement that boasts of supernatural healings, visions, dreams and tongues. But my point is very simple. Bible miracles are invariably *spectacular, undeniable* and *obvious to all*. The

healing of the lame man in Acts 3 caused
widespread amazement (v. 10) could not be denied
(4:16), and was completely open for all to see (3:16;
4:14). Contrast this unquestionable demonstration
of divine power with modern "miracles", and one is
struck by their triviality, doubtfulness, and secrecy.
How radically different from the overtly God-
honouring wonders of Scripture!

Those who teach the need for Pentecostal
experiences, themselves signally fail to duplicate
the divine original. Acts 2 records a mighty rushing
wind from heaven (v. 2), a visible display of fiery
tongues (v. 3), and a supernatural ability given to
Galilean disciples to speak fluently in foreign
languages (v. 4). Not only do charismatics fail to
reproduce the first two phenomena, they also lack
the third. Notice carefully: at Pentecost, God
assembled a multitude of non-Palestine Jews (v. 5)
who could identify the languages supernaturally
spoken by the disciples, thus authenticating a
remarkable miracle. Modern tongue-speaking con-
sists, not in genuine languages, but in ecstatic
babble—meaningless, pointless, and certainly not a
glorious display of divine power.

In the very area of which the charismatic makes
his boast, he fails to pass the Scriptural test. His
"miracles" are just nothing like those in the Word.

3. It Elevates Experience above Scripture. The
charismatic obsession with special gifts, experiences
and sensations is highly dangerous because it
ultimately diverts the believer's attention away
from the solid, immutable truth of the Word. A
Christian life built on the primacy of feelings will be

only as strong and durable as those feelings. But we have something much better as a foundation—the unshakeable rock of Scripture (Matt 7:24).

Notice how Peter moves from his delight in recollecting the unique experience of the transfiguration to a powerful affirmation of the sufficiency of God's Word: "We have also the prophetic word more sure, whereunto ye do well that ye take heed" (2 Pet 1:16-19). To quote Samuel Cox, "Peter knew a sounder basis for faith than that of signs and wonders"[2]; more sure, more certain even than his own tremendous experience was the authority of the written Word of God.

In Luke 24, the Lord Jesus prepared the disciples for His physical absence by pointing them, not to the perpetuation of miracles, but to the Word of truth. At the tomb the women were reminded of His words (vv. 6-8); on the road the Lord Himself instructed from the Scriptures (vv. 25-27); and in the upper room He turned His followers to the Old Testament as the explanation of His own ministry and the authority for theirs (vv. 44-48). The Saviour is made known today, not through signs and wonders, but through the Word of God. That alone will preserve the believer from error (Psa 119:104).

4. It Disregards God's Order. Tongue-speaking is the great charismatic distinguishing mark, the sign of special blessing; and yet even a cursory reading of the only doctrinal examination of the subject in the Bible (1 Cor 12-14) shows how Paul repeatedly demonstrates its relative insignificance. It comes *last* in the two lists of gifts (1 Cor 12:10, 28); and it is far inferior to prophecy (1 Cor 14:4). Further, it is significant that the only tongue-speaking assembly in the New Testament is basically short in godliness, for (and note this carefully) *spiritual gifts do not guarantee spirituality* (1 Cor 3:3).

Again, Paul makes it clear that tongues are *a sign to unbelieving Jews* (1 Cor 14:21, 22), *not* a gift for the upbuilding of the assembly (1 Cor 14:19). When the period of God's governmental dealings with Israel passed with the destruction of Jerusalem in A.D. 70, that sign gift quickly faded away, as history testifies.

The charismatic movement has almost entirely disregarded Paul's teaching, and places first what God has placed last. In the final analysis, its miracles and thrills are a deception, because they do not square with the objective truth of God's Word. The young believer will take the wise counsel of Peter who exhorts us, not to seek experiences, but to "grow in grace and in the knowledge of our Lord and Saviour Jesus Christ" (2 Pet 3:18).

References:
1. W.E. Vine, *Expository Dictionary of N.T. Words*, Vol. 2, p. 147.
2. Quoted in M.R. Vincent, *Word Studies in N.T.* Vol. 1, p. 327.

What Does Separation Mean?

The Lord Jesus made it clear in His High Priestly prayer that while His people are *in* the world they are not *of* the world (John 17:11, 16). That first relationship we can understand well enough: we all live in a society that has rejected God, and rub shoulders daily with folk who do not know the Saviour. And not only is that unavoidable (1 Cor 5:10), it is necessary if we are to reach them for Christ (John 17:18).

At the same time, however, the Christian does not belong to this order of things, and his heavenly citizenship means that he is but an alien and a stranger as far as the affairs of the world are concerned. Our home is in glory, and we await the Master's soon return to take us there (Phil 3:20, 21)! Thus, the Lord's word to His people is that they should be *separate* (2 Cor 6:17) and *distinct* (Phil 2:15, 16) in the midst of surrounding darkness. One of the gravest problems of the current generation is that is is becoming increasingly difficult to distinguish Christians from non-Christians; and I fear that this is *not* because the unsaved are imitating our life-style!

Let us look at a man who was prepared to stand up for his God and be separate. Dan 1 falls naturally into three sections for our analysis.

1. Daniel's Position (vv. 1-7). Suddenly removed from Jerusalem in 605 B.C., the young man Daniel (probably only about 17 years of age) found himself

in a thoroughly alien, godless environment. More
than that, the society around him did its very best
to transform him into a Babylonian. Mark well the
methods it used to corrupt Daniel's mind and
destroy his testimony to the God of Israel. Four
areas of his life were changed: his home (vv. 1, 2),
his education (vv. 3, 4), his diet (v. 5), and his name
(vv. 6, 7). Think of the pressures on a young man to
conform to that new way of life! And the world
today is out to squeeze every young believer into its
sinful, futile, faceless mould (Rom 12:2). The world
cannot stand real Christians, just as it could not
stand the Lord Jesus (John 15:18). Alas, some who
profess to know the Living God eventually capitulate
to its incessant demands. Demas is a solemn, pitiful
warning (2 Tim 4:10).

But Daniel was prepared to be different! The
smile of God meant more to him than the frown of
men. Though his new home might be Babylon, his
heart was in Jerusalem (Dan 6:10); though he might
be put through a three year university course to
brainwash him into the philosophy of an idolatrous
nation, his mind was saturated with the Scriptures
(Dan 9:2); and though they changed his name from
Daniel ("God is my judge") to Belteshazzar ("Bel's
prince"), he consistently refers to himself as "I
Daniel" (Dan 8:15).

Watch out, young Christian! The world will woo
you with promises of wealth and affluence, trying
to make you abandon your pilgrim life and settle
down into materialistic complacency — but remember Matt 6:19, 20: "Lay not up for yourselves
treasures upon earth, where moth and rust doth
corrupt, and where thieves break through and

steal: But lay up for yourselves treasures in heaven". The world will bombard you with its godless evolutionary humanism, mocking your simple faith in the absolute integrity and inerrancy of God's Word — but hold on to Gen 1:1: "In the beginning God created the heaven and the earth".

2. Daniel's Purpose (vv. 8-16). This is one of the great "buts" of the Bible! "But Daniel purposed in his heart that he would not defile himself with the portion of the king's meat, nor with the wine which he drank" (v. 8). Now, notice carefully, we are not told what was wrong with the king's food. Perhaps it had been offered to idols (Exod 34:15); perhaps it contained blood (Lev 3:17); perhaps it was unclean according to Jewish law (Lev 11)—we are not specifically told. And yet Daniel declines it. It is as if he is saying, "There is a potential risk of breaking my God's law if I eat this food, and I want to be on the safe side. Therefore I will not touch any of it".

Now, how narrow can you get? Surely such a fanatical tightness is totally unrealistic! But observe, first, that God honours Daniel's desire to be separate (vv. 9, 15), and, second, that his uncompromising stand influences some other young men, encouraging them to hold on to the truth of God (vv. 11, 12 and 3:16-18). You see, the story of Daniel is a devastating repudiation of the old lie that "narrowness" (if I may use this term of a genuine desire to obey God's Word) necessarily implies ungraciousness (vv. 9, 12, 13 depict Daniel as a winsome young man), isolationism (he finds three like-minded friends!), and evangelistic failure (vv. 14-16). On the contrary, God manifests His unqualified approval of Daniel's separation.

Should we not learn that it is only fitting that believers go out of their way to avoid the slightest suggestion of disobedience to the Lord's commands? Writes Spurgeon: "Daniel determined to go too far rather than not far enough. It is always safest if you are at war with a deadly enemy to have a very high wall between you and him. There will be no fault in its being too high if he aims at destroying you."[1] Apply that to some of those niggling questions of Christian behaviour—should I attend this activity or join that movement? Answer: I am going to be on the safe side and avoid anything that might endanger my Christian testimony. Daniel's principle might even help those saved young women who find it hard to cover their heads in Christian gatherings. *Be on the safe side!* You cannot possibly be wrong in covering your head, but you may be very wrong indeed if you do not (1 Cor 11:1-16). Those who truly love the Lord would rather be safe than sorry.

3. Daniel's Prosperity (vv. 17-21). As we have already seen, God blesses His faithful servant, for "them that honour me I will honour, and they that despise me shall be lightly esteemed" (1 Sam 2:30). The stand that Daniel took as a teenager laid a firm foundation for the rest of his life—and that is why the chapter ends with a summary reference to his long period of service in Babylon (v. 21). Even the world had to recognise the power of God in Daniel's life (v. 19; 2:48).

Daniel is a telling witness to the fact that God's truth cannot be maintained through compromise, and compromise cannot be avoided without separation. Are *you* prepared to be different for God?

Reference:
1. C.H. Spurgeon, *Sermons on the Book of Daniel*, Marshall, Morgan and Scott, 1966, p. 167.

Can The Backslider Be Restored?

The simple answer is yes! Most of us know how easy it is to drift from the Lord Jesus and slip into the ways of a godless world. And yet our God is so gracious that He longs to receive back all who have wandered from His path. That, surely, is the main thrust of the parable of the prodigal son—the backslider's repentance, return, and reception.

But better than restoration is prevention. As a teenager, I occasionally yearned for one of those dramatic conversion experiences which tend (wrongly, I suspect) to be so widely publicised. Then someone wisely suggested to me that it was far better to build a strong fence at the top of the cliff than a hospital at the bottom. And I began to recognise the value of a Christian upbringing. The same applies to backsliding. Although God can and will restore the repentant prodigal, that is no excuse for slack behaviour among young Christians. Like Paul, let us aim to go on for God: "This one thing I do, forgetting those things which are behind, and reaching forth unto those things which are before, I press toward the mark for the prize of the high calling of God in Christ Jesus" (Phil 3:13, 14).

How, then, can the young believer guard against backsliding? First, by learning that it is *never* an overnight disaster, but rather the fruit of an extended period of gradual departure. Its symptoms are many and various, but the disease is always the same: "thou hast left thy first love" (Rev 2:4). A little while ago, a Christian student expressed to me his anxiety over the conflict between Biblical creation and the theory of evolution. Feeling that this was but one indicator of a deeper malaise, I probed further to discover that he had stopped reading the Word and praying. In his case, the creation-evolution problem can wait until he is back in fellowship with the Lord, when he will be in the only sure spiritual position to handle it successfully.

Peter's failure, as recorded in Luke 22, is both an historical record (and how comforting it is to find that such men also had their difficulties!) and a divine warning to us all. Observe Peter's seven steps downwards.

1. Self-Confidence (v. 33). "Lord, I am ready". Poor Peter! That grand assertion of enduring love for the Master, every word of which he sincerely meant, is the start of his decline. The minute we are yet taken up with our love for Christ instead of His love for us, we are in danger. Watch out, young Christian! The devil loves to encourage self-confidence, complacency, a feeling that I am really getting on well spiritually (or, at least, better than many of my friends!). John, on the other hand, calls himself, *not* the disciple who loved Jesus, but "the disciple whom Jesus loved" (John 21:20). Confidence, *not* in the flesh (Phil 3:3), *not* in our brethren (Psa 118:8, 9), but in Christ alone—that is the believer's only resource.

You see, the Christian, although saved for ever by precious blood, is still (yes, even after conversion) a feeble, frail individual, possessed of a deceitful heart (Jer 17:9) and subject to the joint attacks of

Satan (Luke 22:31) and the world (John 15:19).
From first to last, our salvation depends *not on
ourselves* but on the Living God. To quote another:
"It is not what a man does *before* conversion that
saves him; it is not what a man does *after* conversion
that saves him; but salvation is in Christ and of
Christ alone".

This, of course, is basic doctrine. But it needs to
be cherished. We are weak people, but we have an
omnipotent Saviour.

2.   Prayerlessness (vv. 45, 46). If I can manage on
my own, I don't need to pray! Peter was, alas,
consistent in his false self-estimate, and fell asleep
when he should have prayed (Matt 26:40).

Prayer is the most enriching and precious
expression of our relationship with God, and once it
is curtailed, our whole spiritual life suffers. When
the Lord Jesus said, "Men ought always to pray and
not to faint" (Luke 18:1), He was making the point
that if we *don't* pray we *shall* faint! Ponder the
example of Daniel who, with all his government
responsibilities, still made time for regular prayer
(Dan 6:10). That habit did not develop suddenly: it
was the ingrained discipline of many years. Start a
solid prayer life *now*.

3.   Impulsiveness (vv. 49-51). Try to catch the
atmosphere in the garden. The soldiers move to
arrest the Lord—the disciples begin to panic—they
ask if they should resist...and Peter jumps the gun!
Notice, the question comes in verse 49, the answer
in verse 51, and Peter's zealous blunder in verse 50
(compare John 18:10).

Self-assured, out of touch with the Lord, Peter does what he ought not. Understandable as his action may be, it marks the gap between his mind and the Lord's. How much harm in assemblies is caused by hasty action!

4. Distance (v. 54). Scripture reflects Peter's spiritual separation in a physical description — he "followed afar off". Peter is still there, but unwilling to be associated publicly with the despised Nazarene. The Saviour is still despised, and those who stand with him must expect to face the world's scorn. Beware lest fear of man's opinion makes you draw back into the shadows.

5. Wrong Company (v. 55). This is a solemn illustration of Paul's teaching in 2 Cor 6:14-18. And it is probably the biggest single cause of backsliding among young Christians today. If we persistently mix with the world we shall become like the world. Far from lifting the unsaved up to our level, we shall be dragged remorselessly down to theirs. It happened to Lot (Gen 19), to Samson (Jud 16:4-21), to Solomon (1 Kings 11:1-4)...and to Peter. So let us be positive. Keep to the right company! Like the early Christians, we should be linked to an assembly which can be called our "own company" (Acts 4:23). Attend all the meetings—and if you have any spare time, look for other Bible-based activities at nearby assemblies. We all desperately need the fellowship of the saints.

6. Forgetfulness of the Word (vv. 57-60). Would you not have thought that Peter's first denial (v. 57) would have reminded him of the Lord's words in v. 34? But it did not. Only when the Lord looked at him was his sluggish memory stirred (v. 61). When we slip back into the world we tend to forget all the warnings of God's precious Word.

Perhaps it is time for a personal check-up in *your* life. Can you say with the psalmist, "Thy word have I hid in my heart, that I might not sin against thee" (Psa 119:11)?

7. Outright Denial (vv. 57-60). Continual backsliding leads eventually to the abandonment of even an outward profession of Christianity. As the Saviour taught, it is imposible to serve two masters (Matt 6:24). And Peter's position is the logical outcome of that self-confidence in verse 33. "We learn," writes C.H. Mackintosh, "that we cannot trust ourselves for a single moment; for, if not kept by grace, there is no depth of sin into which we are not capable of falling."[1]

The answer? A vote of "no confidence" in self and a whole-hearted cleaving to the Lord, as Barnabas recommends in Acts 11:23. May Peter's example encourage us to walk humbly with our God. You see, *there is no need to backslide!*

Reference:

1. C.H. Mackintosh, *The Mackintosh Treasury*, Loizeaux Bros., 1976, p. 410.

How Can I Witness To Others?

(Part 1)

The other day, while re-reading that sad (and doubtless slanted) account of a Christian home, *Father and Son*, I was struck by the following sentence. It describes the remarkable, unflagging evangelistic zeal of Edmund Gosse's mother:

> "She scarcely ever got into a railway carriage or into an omnibus, without presently offering tracts to the persons sitting within reach of her, or endeavouring to begin a conversation with someone of the sufficiency of the Blood of Jesus to cleanse the human heart from sin."[1]

Would that we were equally fervent! Not some, but *all* saved sinners are commissioned to broadcast the most vital piece of news the world can ever hear. We are "ambassadors for Christ" (2 Cor 5:20), "epistle[s] of Christ" (2 Cor 3:3), "a royal priesthood ...that ye should show forth the excellencies of him who hath called you out of darkness into his marvellous light" (1 Pet 2:9). Yes, evangelism involves us all (Mark 5:19).

Now, although most believers recognise to some extent their personal responsibility as witnesses for the Saviour, not all seem aware of what Scripture says about the nature of our message or the manner of its presentation. Therefore, it is necessary first to outline the fundamentals of the gospel. The importance of getting it absolutely right is evident not merely in Paul's image of the ambassador (for

no government representative has any authority to
alter his instructions) but also in the stern language
of Gal 1:8: "Though we, or an angel from heaven,
preach any other gospel unto you than that which
we have preached unto you, let him be accursed".
Hardly the easy-going vocabulary of ecumenical
compromise or peaceful toleration! But, then, if
salvation is only on God's terms, isn't Paul right to
insist that those terms be presented correctly?
Make no mistake, this is a matter of life and death.
The slightest alteration in a chemist's prescription
may turn a life-saving medicine into a deadly poison
...and any tampering with the fundamentals of "the
gospel of God" (Rom 1:1) will neutralise its divine
power.

Sir Robert Anderson tells of the French Minister
of War who justified his dismissal of a military
officer in these words: "He committed an offence,
and I removed him; he paraphrased an order which
it was his duty only to read."[2] God has entrusted
His people with a specific message—His peace
proposals to a rebel world, we might say—and we
are responsible, not for the reception of that
message, but for its safe and accurate delivery.
Ezek 33:2-9 is a challenging and memorable
illustration of this. And since it is the Lord's
message, the very words used are crucial (2 Cor
2:17; 1 Cor 15:1, 2 R.V.).

Today we face error from two extremes. There
are those who preach what we might call the
Gospel of God *plus,* or the "too much" gospel. That
is, they hold that Calvary is not enough, and has to
be supplemented by sacraments, good works,
ritual, charismatic experiences, or whatever, before

salvation is guaranteed. But this contradicts Eph 2:8, 9 which insists that salvation is *by grace through faith plus nothing.*

> "Nothing in my hand I bring,
> Simply to Thy cross I cling."

At the other end of the scale is the popular evangelist who proclaims the Gospel of God *minus,* or the "too little" gospel. This is characterised by the absence of certain truths which might prove offensive, such as the unspeakable holiness of God, man's total sinfulness, and the reality of hell. Such a streamlined gospel, often accompanied by entertainment which smacks more of the world than the church of God, sounds very shallow when measured against Paul's great exposition of salvation truth in Romans. You see, God's Word is so precious that, when proclaiming it, the believer must make sure that he handles "the truth, the whole truth, and nothing but the truth".

What, then, is the gospel we preach, whether we are on a platform, or simply talking with our friends? Four crucial elements are found in Romans 5:1-11.

1. Sin (v. 8) = Ruin. Paul makes it plain that, without Christ, our condition is desperate. Notice the words he uses. We are "without strength" (v. 6), that is to say, *weak.* We are "ungodly" (v. 6), positively contrary to all that God is, and therefore deliberately *wilful* in our disobedience. We are "sinners" (v. 8), shooting so far short of the divine target of perfection as to be inexcusably *wayward.* Finally, we are "enemies" (v. 10), rebels against the living God, *at war* with our Creator.

All this means utter ruin. Not a minor fault, or a slight problem, but absolute disaster. Spell it out clearly, faithfully and lovingly, for only a sinner needs a Saviour. And Romans 1-3 hammers home the unpalatable truth that *all*, however respectable, are "under sin" (Rom 3:9).

2. Wrath (v. 9) = Retribution. This solemn word refers to the righteous anger of a holy God against all that pollutes His universe, and it is an indispensible part of the gospel. How tragic, then, when evangelists remain criminally silent about the reality of hell, or, worse still, trivialise it! Contrast the example of the greatest of all preachers who, before speaking about the certainty of judgment, first wept over those who were heading for it (Luke 19:41-44). The "should not perish" of John 3:16 reminds us that the gospel cannot be preached without mentioning judgment.

Don't misunderstand me. I believe firmly in the love of God so gloriously displayed at Calvary. But that love can never be fully appreciated until we see that God is also the holy, righteous Judge, and that we deserve nothing but eternal hell. Paul reveals God's wrath (Rom 1:16-18; 2:5, 6) before proclaiming His love (Rom 5:8).

3. Blood (v. 9) = Remedy. God's remedy for sin—the *only* remedy—is the precious blood of Christ. "Hell" and "blood" are unpopular words, but they are both in the Book. Of course, to understand what Scripture means by blood we must study the Old Testament, and we shall come to the conclusion that in the context of Rom 5 it signifies *a sacrificial* *death which allows God righteously to forgive sinners* (Heb 9:22). Simply to preach that Christ died is inadequate; we must explain *why* He died, and *what* that death means to God. Paul's message, you'll notice, is that "Christ died for our sins *according to the scriptures*" (1 Cor 15:3). Without the doctrinal explanation we have no gospel.

Don't be afraid to preach that forgiveness is available only through the shed blood of Christ. After all, it will be our song for eternity (Rev 5:9)!

4. Faith (v. 1) = Responsibility. All man-made religion, from Cain onwards, is demolished by that one word "faith". It allows no room for human effort, for "works of righteousness which we have done" (Titus 3:5), for reformation, for tears, for ritual observances. God demands nothing but my whole-hearted confidence for eternity in the sacrifice of the Lord Jesus Christ for me. God says it: I believe it: that settles it!

Young Christian, check your message carefully. Make sure that it is "the gospel of God", no more and no less. And then, like Paul, so selflessly devoted to the truth, you may be able to call it "my gospel" (2 Tim 2:8).

References:
1. Edmund Gosse, *Father and Son*, Penguin Books, 1972, p.42.
2. Sir Robert Anderson, *Redemption Truths*, John Ritchie, n.d., p.112.

How Can I Witness to Others?

(Part 2)

Having considered the essentials of the gospel message itself, let us now look at what the Bible says about our manner of presentation. The basic principle to grasp is that *God's work is always best done in God's way.*

The Master's Speech. The Lord Jesus Christ is our perfect example for all Christian activity (1 Cor 11:1), so it will be helpful to consider how He spoke to people. Four characteristics emerge.

1. Authority. "The multitudes were astonished at his doctrine: for he taught them as one having authority, and not as the scribes" (Matt 7:28, 29). In His words the Lord had a personal power which startled the Jews. His repeated "I say unto you" indicated a unique authority. While we do not possess that distinct attribute of the Son of God, we do carry a divine message that should be proclaimed with certainty and conviction. "If any man speak, let him speak as the oracles of God" (1 Pet 4:11). Thus, when Paul evangelised Thessalonica, his gospel was received "not as the word of man, but as it is in truth, the word of God" (1 Thess 2:13).

Mind you, authority is not to be confused with arrogance. Our message is based squarely on the infallible Word, but we ourselves are only sinners saved by grace. Someone has said that evangelism is merely one beggar telling another beggar where to find bread. In ourselves we have nothing to be proud of—but we do know where that life-giving bread is! Let us say so with conviction (Psa 107:2).

2. Simplicity. This is another feature of the Lord's teaching, proving beyond doubt that "deep truth" (or whatever we want to call it) need not be unintelligible! The Master's use of parables, common-place objects and activities to shed light on spiritual realities, is a lesson for every preacher.

Does it not follow that if child-like faith is the qualification for entrance into the kingdom of heaven (Matt 18:3), then the gospel itself must be clear enough for a child to grasp? "Thou hast hid these things from the wise and prudent, and hast revealed them unto babes" (Matt 11:25). May we keep our message so simple that the humblest listener will be able to understand it.

"Make the message clear and plain:
Christ receiveth sinful men."

3. Sincerity. There was an evident genuineness about the Lord Jesus. The deep reality of His love and compassion for souls shone through all He said and did. "When he saw the multitudes, he was moved with compassion on them, because they fainted, and were scattered abroad, as sheep having no shepherd" (Matt 9:36). We might have seen that huge crowd as a nuisance, a faceless mass of humanity, perhaps even as a threat. The Lord saw them as lost sheep, and His good shepherd's heart responded to their need. There was nothing unfeelingly automatic or routine about His ministry to men and women.

While our gospel message should be as clear and

accurate as the BBC News (indeed more so!), its
delivery should be very different. The story of
God's love for a world of lost sinners cannot be
presented with the cool detachment of an academic
lecture. It must move the speaker's heart, as it did
the Lord's (Matt 23:37) and Paul's (Acts 20:31).

4. Urgency. All the Saviour's activity displayed a
consciousness of the brevity of time (John 4:35;
9:4). The gospel is not a cosy word to be shelved
until a "convenient season" (Acts 24:25) comes
around with nothing better to do. It is an immediate
challenge to the heart. This is why the Lord spoke
solemnly and repeatedly about the eternal judgment
awaiting all who reject Him.

Our evangelism should be marked by urgency,
for "it is time to seek the Lord" (Hosea 10:12). After
we have been snatched up to meet the Lord in the
air there will be no more opportunity to reach the
lost. Much we shall enjoy in eternity, but one
blessing at least will be denied us—the joy of
leading a sinner to Christ. That is a work for *now*.

The Master's Strategy. The Lord Jesus provides not
only an ideal example of gospel testimony but also a
detailed plan of campaign for His servants to follow
while He is personally absent. This strategy is
outlined in Matthew 28:18-20.

1. The Divine Plan. "Go ye therefore". Every child
of God is commissioned to be a gospel witness by
his *walk* (Phil 1:27) and his *talk* (Phil 2:16).

2. The Divine Pattern (vv. 18-20). Make disciples,

baptise them, and instruct them in all the teachings of the Lord Jesus Christ. Sometimes we hear Christians say that the main thing is to see people saved. That may sound reasonable, but it is *not* God's gospel strategy. God's pattern is to see folk saved, baptised, added to a company of believers meeting in accordance with New Testament principles, and continually built up in divine truth. Anything short of this is disobedience to the Great Commission. So let's measure our service against this clear standard. Is *your* gospel activity designed to channel converts into a local assembly? I know a Christian couple who labour conscientously among young people, and yet, tragically, their effort is not associated with an assembly. Its long term value is therefore in grave doubt because it is not doing God's work in God's way.

3. The Divine Power (v. 20). "I am with you always". The believer's faith rests not in the charisma of a powerful speaker, or in clever arguments, or in exciting entertainment, or in an emotional atmosphere. It rests solely in *the power of God*. Read carefully 1 Cor 2:1-5 to see Paul's evangelistic method. The gospel of God does not need gimmicks or showmanship. Indeed, such things (be they dramatic sketches or musical interludes) are at best unnecessary, and at worst, harmful, for they detract from the glory that belongs to God alone.

Let us then by all means reach out with the gospel of the grace of God, but let us make sure that we do it in such a way as to bring honour to the God of our salvation.

How Can I Keep Going?

Quite recently a number of young believers have confessed to me such a feeling of failure in their Christian lives that they wonder if it is worth going on. I cannot quote their exact words, but they amounted to this: "I seem to have fallen so often that it just isn't worth trying any more. And I sometimes wonder if it really makes sense to be a Christian at all".

Sad words these. They remind me of the newly-redeemed Israelites who, facing the first obstacle in their pilgrimage, the pursuing Egyptians, immediately gave way to despair: "Because there were no graves in Egypt, hast thou taken us away to die in the wilderness?...it had been better for us to serve the Egyptians" (Exod 14:11, 12).

In such times of distress and doubt the remedy for us is much as it was for Israel. They needed a backward glance to the *Passover Lamb,* that marvellous token of God's redeeming grace which had purchased them for Himself. Had not the Lord declared, "Sanctify unto me all the firstborn...it is mine" (Exod 13:2)? Who could believe that after such a mighty deliverance God would abandon or fail His people? Likewise, Paul takes us back to Calvary as the index of God's love for His saints: "He that spared not his own Son, but delivered him up for us all, how shall he not with him also freely give us all things?" (Rom 8:32, and see Rom 5:9, 10). In times of difficulty, take a long, wondering look at the cross where our Passover Lamb was slain. Calvary proves the infinite loving kindness of our God.

But Israel should also have looked up. Poised majestically over the camp was the guiding cloud of the divine presence, a cloud which had led them into the very cul-de-sac that seemed now to spell disaster (Exod 13:21, 22). Humanly speaking, their situation was impossible. But the *Pillar of Light* had brought them there. Persecution at work, at school and at home, temptations to return to the old unconverted ways—these things are not pleasant, but they are used by God to toughen us up, to turn us into people who can endure the storms. So look up! Our pillar of light (God's Word) directs our steps daily (Psa 119:105), and although it may lead us up Hill Difficulty it also guarantees the abiding company of the Saviour (Heb 13:5). Whatever happens, follow the Book as faithfully (but *not* as complainingly) as Israel followed the cloud.

One more point. Had Israel but pondered the Lord's words they would have found such encouragement. Listen: "it shall be when the Lord shall bring thee into the land..." (Exod 13:5). How precious! Not only had God brought them *out* (Exod 12:51), He swore to lead them *in.* On the basis of those simple words the thoughtful Israelite could confidently anticipate the *Promised Land.* We too can look ahead to the sure fulfilment of the Lord's promise in John 14:3.

A favourite verse of mine is Phil 1:6, which reads (in the R.V.) "Being confident of this very thing, that He which began a good work in you will perfect it until the day of Jesus Christ". So often we take up a task (perhaps a local assembly responsibility) and then abandon it when our enthusiasm wanes or

problems arise. But not our God! What He begins
He always finishes. *All* those redeemed by precious
blood will be presented "faultless before the
presence of His glory with exceeding joy" (Jude 24).

The first step for the disillusioned believer is to
get the right perspective by looking back, up and
forwards. But what then? Clearly we must go on
for God. 1 Peter 2:1-5 prescribes four essentials for
Christian growth.

1. Give Up (v. 1). The believer, born again through
God's pure Word, cannot continue in impure
practices. As these are exposed by the searchlight of
Scripture they must be confessed and forsaken (Psa
139:23, 24).

Such a narrow outlook is, of course, entirely
foreign to the broad-minded indulgence of a world
which tolerates any evil. But the Christian should
be broad-minded enough to receive *all* of God's
truth (much "liberal" teaching among assemblies
today is, paradoxically, far too narrow because it
resists the full range of Biblical revelation), and
narrow-minded enough to reject *all* error. The
bravest man is he who can say "No" even when the
whole world says "Yes".

If I seem trapped in the treadmill of failure, it may
be because I have not yet said "No" to what God
condemns.

2. Grow Up (v. 2). The only evidence of life is
growth. When D.L. Moody said that converts
should be weighed, not counted, he was wisely
distinguishing between "decisions" and "disciples".
Peter explains the means of growth as the Word.

But remember: an accurate description of the contents of a milk bottle will never in itself promote growth. We have to drink the milk! Likewise, the Word must be appropriated rather than merely analysed. And that is a very personal thing. You see, it is sadly possible to know the truth, even to teach the truth, and yet not to practise it.

Let Jeremiah be our model: "Thy words were found, and I did eat them; and thy word was unto me the joy and rejoicing of mine heart" (Jer 15:16). We shall only keep growing as we feed daily on God's "pure spiritual milk".

3. Build Up (v. 5). Although Peter is writing here about the universal church, it will not be amiss to take his words as an encouragement to build up the local assembly. Certainly we are all building something into our assembly, be it good or ill (1 Cor 3:12), and we shall be judged according to the quality of our work.

Much of the misery and discontent among young Christians today is a result of ecclesiastical laziness —they are not entering whole-heartedly into their assembly activities. Since each of us has a vital role to play, let us do it well. Young man, are you feeling your responsibility as one to whom public prayer and praise are committed (1 Tim 2:8)? Young woman, are you following the pattern of godly women like Phoebe, Priscilla, and Dorcas, whose service to the Lord's people caused their names to be preserved?

If I am to keep going with the Lord, I *must* build up my assembly.

4. Offer Up (v. 5). Every saint is a priest with the privilege of offering to God those sacrifices that delight Him—our persons (Rom 12:1), possessions (Heb 13:16) and praises (Heb 13:15). But a sacrifice is, by definition, costly. Can I suggest that one reason why some believers seem so unsettled is that they have never had to pay a price for their faith?

What does it cost *you* to be a Christian? The jeers of friends, the effort of attending meetings, the time spent in Bible study, money given to the Lord's work? Such sacrifices bring pleasure to God because they are associated with Calvary (compare Phil 4:18 and Eph 5:2). The master said, "Whosoever will lose his life for my sake shall find it" (Matt 16:25), for no one has ever lost out by yielding all to Christ.

Are you going on with God? If you have slipped and fallen, don't lie there in self-pity. Be like the boy who, when asked how he learned to skate so well, replied, "I got up every time I fell down". Get up —and then *go on!*

How Should I Prepare for
The Lord's Supper?

There can be no doubt that the most significant gathering of Christians is when we meet to remember the Lord Jesus as He specially requested. Indeed, although the New Testament makes reference to meetings for prayers (Acts 12:12), Bible teaching (Acts 19:9, 10), missionary reports (Acts 14:26, 27) and evangelism (Acts 18:4), the only meeting for which detailed directions are given is the Lord's Supper (1 Cor 11:2 to 14:40).

If this simple remembrance of the Lord Jesus is so important that it merits specific instructions, and so precious to the Lord Himself that He deliberately instituted it on the eve of His atoning death, how solemn and serious should be our preparation for it! It is a general rule in life that the more we put into something the more we are likely to get out of it. Perhaps one reason I am not appreciating the meetings of my assembly is that I am not coming in the right condition of heart.

How can a young Christian prepare for the remembrance feast? We can glean some ideas from Peter's teaching in his first letter about the Christian priesthood, for (and mark this carefully) every believer is a priest with all the rich privileges and responsibilities this involves. In the Old Testament one family alone was entrusted with the service of God in the Tabernacle. Today the youngest and simplest believer has immediate

access into God's presence through the finished
work of Calvary (Heb 10:19-25), for we are all
priests on the basis of new birth (1 Pet 1:23).
Although this is by no means restricted to assembly
gatherings, it is true that as a priesthood "we offer
up spiritual sacrifices" to our God. What are the
qualifications for effective priestly service?

1. The Priest must be fit (1 Pet 2:1). "Wherefore
laying aside all malice, and all guile, and hypocrisies,
and envies, and all evil speakings". This is a divine
prescription for spiritual health. You see, I cannot
rush into God's holy presence regardless of my
inner condition and expect Him to accept my
worship.

The Old Testament shows in picture form how
vital it is for the priest to be fitted for his holy
duties. In Lev 8 he is first *cleansed* (v. 6)—speaking of
that initial "washing of regeneration" (Titus 3:5)
we receive at conversion; next, he is *clothed* (v. 13)—
just as the believer is made acceptable to God in
Christ (Eph 1:4); and finally he is *consecrated* (v. 24).
Don't forget the meaning of that blood! The
evidence of a sacrifice offered is applied to the
priest's ear, thumb, and toe, showing that "nothing
should enter into the mind, no act be performed,
nothing should be found in their walk through the
world, which should not be according to the
precious blood of Jesus".[1]

No wonder Paul underlines the importance of
self-judgment before participation in the Lord's
Supper. "Not discerning the Lord's body" (1 Cor
11:29) involves a failure to understand the deep
significance of the cross and its claims upon the

believer's whole life. And the penalty for such a
failure may be the most solemn: "For this cause
many are weak and sickly among you, and many
sleep [=have died]" (1 Cor 11:30). This, of course, is
fatherly discipline *not* eternal damnation. Our God
is so unspeakably holy that He cannot permit His
redeemed ones to approach Him without first
judging sin.

Graciously, He provided a visual-aid of self-
examination and cleansing in the Tabernacle. Each
time priests entered the Holy Place to serve the
Lord they had to wash at the laver, "that they die
not" (Exod 30:20). Let us take time regularly at the
laver of God's Word to judge ourselves and put
things right before we seek to remember the
Saviour at His Supper (Matt 5:23, 24).

2. The Priest must be fed (1 Pet 2:2). If the former
verse speaks of my *spiritual condition,* this suggests
the need for *scriptural comprehension.* Only if we are
feeding daily on the Word will we be equipped to
remember the Lord acceptably.

That repeated refrain of whole-hearted obedience,
"as the Lord commanded Moses" (Lev 8:9, 13, 17
etc.) is tragically altered in Lev 10:1, "which He
commanded them *not*". Right at the beginning of
the Jewish priesthood comes failure as two priests
disobey the divine instructions. Our priestly
service is inextricably tied up with obedience to the
Word, for worship must be "in spirit and in truth"
(John 4:24).

As is often said, 1 Cor 11 points our gaze in five
directions. We should look *backwards* to the Lord's
death (v. 26), *upwards* to His present exaltation (v

8

23—for Paul received his information directly from the risen Christ), *forwards* to His coming (v. 26), *inwards* to check our spiritual state (v. 28), and *around* to recognise our oneness with the saints who join us in our remembrance (v. 33). Therefore we need to turn to Scripture to have our minds and hearts fed with such divine truths. When it comes to worship (or any other Christian activity, for that matter), we can only offer to God what we have first received from Him (1 Chron 29:14). And that means prayerful study. My appreciation of the Lord's Supper will be in proportion to my reading of the Word during the preceding week. Young believer, how do you spend your Saturday evenings? Be sure, what we fill our minds with then will influence our worship the following morning.

3. The Priest's hands must be filled (1 Pet 2:3-5). Peter makes it clear that our focus of attention is the Lord Jesus, for our worship indicates our *satisfaction with Christ.* He is the Lord whose goodness we taste (v. 3), the precious corner stone of God's temple (v. 4), and the mediator who makes all our service acceptable to the Father (v. 5). In coming to break bread our prime concern is not to meet the saints, pray for the lost, or even sit under the ministry of the Word. First and foremost we come to give the Saviour His place of absolute pre-eminence.

The Old Testament priests approached God with their hands full of that which spoke of His dear Son (Lev 8:25-27). This illustrates our responsibility. Although God has entrusted the task of audible praise to the men (1 Tim 2:8), the Christian woman is just as valuable to the Lord in her silent adoration—and indeed, many a dear sister has attained a level of worship far above that of the brethren (John 12:1-7). So don't forget: whether we are male or female our heart condition and our Biblical intelligence are an inestimable influence on the tone of the gathering.

In our preparation, let us make sure that we concentrate on Christ, for it is Him we aim to remember. Good hymns can be useful expressions of worship directing our thoughts towards the excellencies of God's Son, but they must be carefully chosen. I recall a brother in my home assembly who always seemed able to select the right hymn at the right time—and that was because he had taken the trouble to get to know the hymn book.

A word to the young men. It is a daunting business to get up for the first time in your own assembly, and all thoughtful elders appreciate this. Nevertheless, I feel that some young men remain silent for so long that they are in danger of joining the tragically numerous ranks of the silent old men! A student faithfully attended our local assembly in Glasgow for five years without ever opening his mouth at the Lord's Supper, and I eventually suggested to him that (unlike some brethren who suffer from the opposite problem) he was coming to the meeting resolved *not* to take part. A better policy is this: come ready but not determined to participate.

You see, worship is not easy. Precisely because it is the believer's highest occupation it demands his utmost in preparation.

Reference:

1. J.N. Darby, *Expository Vol. 1*, p. 240.